FARNLEY
A HISTORY

CAROLINE PAGE

HONLEY CIVIC SOCIETY

FARNLEY TYAS A HISTORY

Published in England by Honley Civic Society

Printed by Enterprise Print, Honley

© Caroline Page and Honley Civic Society

Text Caroline Page

Design PFM

First published 2015
ISBN-13 978-0-9572638-8-8

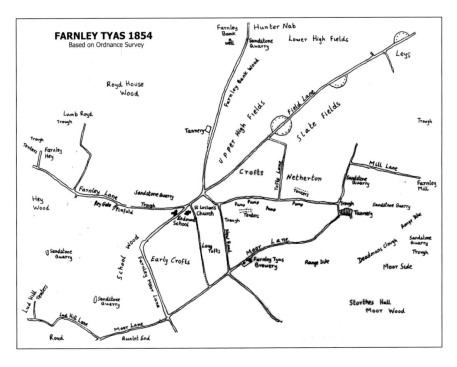

Map of Farnley Tyas based on the 1854 Ordnance Survey map
(Courtesy Huddersfield Local Studies Library)

All spellings and punctuations etc. shown as quotations have been reproduced from the sources as they appear in the original documents.

Some images in this volume have been digitally altered to remove blemishes and correct colour balance.

FARNLEY TYAS A HISTORY

1. INTRODUCTION

The village of Farnley Tyas, in the parish of Almondbury, lies five kilometres south east of Huddersfield, in the shadow of Castle Hill and close to Honley and Thurstonland. It stands at 246 metres above sea level. The village is noted for its scenic beauty comprising meadows and woodlands, vernacular buildings of local stone and wild flowers and birds. It is especially beautiful in the springtime when the woodlands are carpeted with bluebells. There are about 130 properties within the Village and the population is about 300.

Possible explanations for the origins of the name 'Farnley Tyas' are either 'lea of the ferns' or 'the far lea'. 'Fearn' is Old English for fern and 'leah' is a lea or meadow. Possibly 'Farnley' describes a clearing overgrown with ferns. There are several villages in Yorkshire called Farnley and to avoid confusion with them the local village acquired the distinguishing affix Tyas. So, in Farnley Tyas we have a Saxon place-name (Farnley) coupled with the family name of the occupiers (Tyas from Teutonicus).

2. A GHOST STORY - RIMMINGTON'S GHOST

Farnley Tyas people who are born in the village are called 'Robinets'. In 2015, two people can claim this title: Peggy Dodson was born in 1925 in Farnley Tyas and Vera Cocking who was born in 1928 at Wood Farm below Hunter's Nab. The origin of this tradition lies in a ghost which is said to haunt Woodsome Hall.

In the latter part of the seventeenth century James Rimmington was the steward of the estate. He married Sarah Kay in 1683; she came from Farnley Tyas and was a maid at Woodsome Hall. The story goes that James was feared and hated by everyone. When he died in December 1697, the Farnley villagers looked forward to a more peaceful time and few were sorry to see him go due to his harsh ways. Unfortunately for them, their joy was short-lived as his ghost continued the ways of the former tyrant. It struck terror into one Farnley Tyas resident who met it galloping on horseback down Woodsome Lane accompanied by a couple of hounds. Another resident complained that the ghost had plucked a nail from a door post while passing a house at the bottom of the village street. Eventually the persecutions became so intolerable that an appeal was made to the local clergy to put the wandering spirit to rest. It was finally laid in Rimmington's Chamber at Woodsome Hall, there to remain as long as the hollins (the holly trees) remained green. Strange noises were heard from this room. Another version of the story is that the ghost was changed into a robin redbreast which haunts the holly trees. This latter version explains why Farnley Tyas people are called 'Robinets'. There is said to be a tunnel, or subterranean passage, leading from the Hall to the little valley in front, attributed to Mr. Rimmington.

It should be added that the story may not be true and that it has given James Rimmington a reputation which he hardly deserves; he was a just and faithful steward of the Kays and a true friend of the tenants (*Huddersfield Examiner 18th June, 1938*).

3. LANDOWNERS AND LORDS OF THE MANOR AT FARNLEY

The earliest reference to Farnley Tyas is in the Domesday Book of 1086 in which brief mention is made of Fereleia. Until 1066 the Lords of the manor were Godwin and Swein and, after the Norman Conquest, the Lord in 1086 was Ilbert de Lacy. 'Ilbert has it now, but it is waste. Godwin and Swein had 3 carucates of land to be taxed; where 3 ploughs might be employed. The value to the Lord in the time of King Edward (the

Tombstone with the inscription 'The noble knight Baldwin Tyas [Nobilis miles Baldwinius Teutonicus]' with permission of D Bagley

Confessor) was 40s. There was woodland pasture 6 furlongs long and 6 broad'. (The carucate, or ploughland, was a unit of assessment for tax. It was based on the area a plough team of eight oxen could till in a ploughing season: about 120 acres).

After the Norman Conquest all land in England was owned by the King, William 1, who then distributed it to those who had helped him in the overthrow of the Saxons. He gave the northern manor of Farnley to Ilbert de Lacy who built Pontefract Castle. A descendant, Henri de Lacy, passed these lands to his nephew, Gilbert de Notton, at the end of the 1100s. Between 1210 and 1234 they were passed to Roger de Notton.

By 1236 the Farnley lands had been inherited, through marriage, by Baldwin Teutonicus; his name was later shortened to Tyas. Thus, Tyas was the name of a family which held land in the neighbourhood in the thirteenth century. Franco Tyas was the grandson of Baldwin Teutonicus and he followed his father as Lord of the Manor around 1260. 'Tieis' was the old French word for German. Canon Hulbert (*The Annals of the Church and Parish of Almondbury, 1880 p.187*) states 'the family of Tyas, calling themselves in Latin Teutonici, appear to have been magnificent persons. Sir Baldwin Teutonicus is called 'a noble knight' in ancient records'. Baldwin Teutonicus was buried in the church of St. Mary's in the deserted village of Lead, near Tadcaster.

From 1200 to 1400 the name Tyas occurs with great regularity in subsidy rolls (records of taxation), land deeds and court rolls in the Parish of Almondbury. In 1379 the Poll Tax lists John Tyas as a resident of Farnley, paying only four pence, indicating a reduction in the family's status. The evidence which survives for the next 150 years suggests that the Tyas's were very little different from many other local yeoman families. They lived close to their original homes. More recently, Tyas families have been living in the Kirkburton and Almondbury parishes for the last four-hundred years (*Redmonds, G. Huddersfield Examiner 8th April, 1974*).

Franco Tyas left the Manor of Woodsome and Farnley to William Finchenden in 1370; from 1370-1378 the knightly family of Finchenden held the Manor. An indenture (contract) dated 1378 stated that 'Dame Alyce Fynchenden grants to John Cay her Manor of Woodsome, including Farnley Tyas'. From this time the Farnley estates remained in the ownership of the Kaye family. There are numerous references to members of the family living in the area.

The 1379 the Poll Tax lists John Kay, yeoman, as a resident of Farnley and taxed at 40d; the rest at four pence. The levy was at the rate of four pence upon each person over the age of 16 years. The collectors' returns recorded that there were ten adult males and 11 adult females inhabiting Farnley Tyas (*Sykes, D.F.E. 1898 p.141*).

The Dartmouth Estate Deeds (*Kirklees Archives*) contain a reference to a marriage settlement of the son of Laurence Kay involving land at Farnley Tyas and dated 26th July, 1420. There are also documents of settlements, leases, transfers of land, houses and outbuildings all dating from the middle of the 1400s, all mentioning the Kay family of Woodsome and land at Farnley Tyas.

The Kay family appears again in records from the time of Henry VIII. In 1523 the Commons granted a subsidy upon lands, goods and wages to the King. This was to enable him to wage the war with France 'for the conservation of his honour, and for the avenging of the wrongs to his highness and his subjects'.

The returns of the collectors for 'Fernelay Tyas' were:

William Rischworth	Tax 5s 0d
Charles Cay	Tax 4s 0d
Thurston Cay	Tax 1s 0d
Thomas Snappe	Tax 1s 0d

(Sykes, D. F. E. 1898 p.145)

In 1726 the heir to the Woodsome and Farnley estate, Sir Arthur Kaye of Woodsome, died without a male heir and the family's extensive estates passed to the Earl of Dartmouth whose son, George Legge, (son of the first Earl of Dartmouth) had married Sir Arthur's only child, Elizabeth, in 1722. Thus ownership of the Farnley Tyas estate changed from the Kaye family to the Dartmouth family.

4. EARLY LIFE IN FARNLEY TYAS

Manor Court Rolls of Woodsome with Farnley Tyas 1381–1684

The records of the manorial courts start in the mid-13th century; the practice of keeping manorial records became widespread as landlords copied the example of the king's court. Every lord of the manor had the right to hold a court for his tenants who farmed tenanted land on their own behalf, paying rents and services to the lord in return for their use of the land. Whether or not freeholders attended the manorial courts depended on local practice.

The manorial courts were an important source of income for the lord. Money flowed into the lord's coffers, particularly in the form of 'amercements' (fines), from tenants infringing the lord's rights and privileges.

Records were kept of the activities of a manorial court; they describe the daily lists of business which were scheduled to appear in courts and these regulated a wide range of aspects of life and commerce. The 'pains' were the regulations issued by the jury of a manorial court, the breach of which incurred a fixed penalty. The regulations involved, for example, the organisation of communal agriculture, the scouring of ditches, the use of public wells, the control of animals etc. The records allow us to eavesdrop on the everyday world of those distant times in the late middle ages and they give us a glimpse of the concerns and activities of Farnley Tyas people. They tell us about rural agricultural life, its hardships and the pervasive control of the lord of the manor who exercised jurisdiction over his tenants. Quotations from the manorial court rolls give significant insights into this period of history.

In 1381 Richard II was king of England. He overcame a rebel army during the Peasants' Revolt but surrendered the throne in 1399 to Henry IV; Richard was imprisoned at Pontefract Castle where he died in 1400. The manorial court rolls of Woodsome with Farnley Tyas for 1381 show that while these national events were taking place life in Farnley Tyas was far removed from the activities of Richard II.

Building work

'Thomas Cubbock has a day until the next court to roof his grange' (a manor used for food production). 'Edward Brodehede shall build and repair his house sufficiently before the Feast of Saint Martin next coming...'. It was seen as an offence against the stability of the community to allow houses and buildings to fall into decay.

Management

'William Bythelane was elected Reeve of Farnley this year' (manager of a manor and overseer of the peasants).

Controlling livestock

The control of animals was important in this farming community. In the earliest records, dating from 1381, it is stated that 'Thomas Fideler complains of William Bythelane about a plea of trespass with his sheep. He has grazed the oats in the land of the said Thomas with damage to the land...'. 'John Kay complains of Thomas Cubbock on a plea of trespass and says with his beasts he has grazed on the hay of the said John and he has broken the walls of a certain dwelling causing damage.....the said Thomas has admitted this...'.

About 100 years later, in the time of Henry VIII, England was moving from Catholicism to Protestantism. However, the manorial court rolls of Farnley Tyas record that the tenants were experiencing problems with stray animals. In 1524 it is recorded that 'A pain has been set for the tenants of Farnley that they should make the pynfold at Farnley before the Feast of John the Baptist...'. A pinfold is a circular enclosure completely walled around with a gateway for entrance which could be securely fastened.

In 1566, it was reported that 'John Butherode has unlawfully chased his neighbour's sheep with his dogs...'. In 1568 'Everyone should put his pigs under yoke at the May Day and get them ringed at the Feast of Michael and keep them so...'. In 1572 'An injunction was made that no one should put any geese into the fields that have been sown until all the grain be removed...'. In 1598 ' George Harpyn has eaten other people's grass with his sheep' and 'William Tyas, Henry Lynthwaite and Richard Kay with their cattle have eaten the lord's wood'.

Straying animals must have been common and in 1598 we can find a link to the 1524 regulation, made in the reign of Henry VIII, that Farnley tenants should build a 'pynfold'. 'An injunction was made in 1598 for the inhabitants of this manor that they should make the lord's fold (a pen for animals) satisfactory with walls and with a key and wax before the Feast of the Nativity of St. John the Baptist next coming...'.

The pinfold as seen today, viewed from Honley Road

A pinder was an official appointed by the Manor Court whose duties were to collect the stray animals and pen, or impound, them inside the 'pynfold' – Before allowing any animal to be released the pinder imposed a fine. The ruins of the pinfold can still be seen today.

Keeping sheep on the common

Regulations were enforced concerning the number of sheep which could be kept on the common land and there were many transgressors 'Richard Marsh is overburdening the lord's common with his sheep... he should relieve that common of the burden before the Feast of the Nativity of John the Baptist...'. In 1598, we read 'A pain is laid for all the inhabitants and tenants of this manor that none of them should keep more sheep on the common after seven days than by right he ought to have and to keep in accordance with the size of his holding and the rate set at a limit for him...'. In 1601 there is another reference to a tenant who has 'overburdened the common with his sheep".

Draught animals

In 1550, during the reign of Edward VI, who favoured the religious ideas of the Protestant Reformation, in Farnley Tyas the consequences of the break with Rome did not appear to have much impact on everyday life.

The manorial court roll on 4th November, 1550 records other concerns of the yeoman farmers 'Edward Ainley and others...put their draught animals (strong working animals, such as oxen or mules, used to draw a load like a cart or a plough) on the common where they ought to have no right of common'. Draught animals were causing problems again in 1560. The jurors stated that 'draught animals were on the Common where they have no right and they have consumed their neighbour's grass with their draught animals".

Cutting timber

After the Wars of the Roses, in 1498, while Henry VII was consolidating the Crown, having won at Bosworth, and healing the wounds after the thirty year civil war by marrying Elizabeth of York, in Farnley Tyas it was recorded that 'John Wood, Oliver Copley and William Airton have cut down and carried away green wood and underwood of the lord without license therefore each one of them for his part is in amercement…'(the fine for the offence).tenants in 1606, in the reign of James I, were also 'amerced of the lord for carrying off greenwood from the lord's wood without license…cutting down young oaks in the lord's wood…'. This was an infringement of the lord's rights.

Maintaining fences and hedges

In 1524 'An injunction (was) given to the tenants of Farnley that they should make up their hedges and fences between themselves and the lord and keep them so repaired…'. This is a reference to the enclosures of the sixteenth century which changed the nature of farming and the look of the land.

In 1550 it was reported that 'Henry Parkyn has not got his hedges sufficiently repaired…'. In 1566 'An injunction was made that everyone shall keep up his hedges and doles (boundaries) round the corn that has been sown on the moor up to the feast of Michael…'. In 1568 'An injunction was made for John Dolyff and Robert Hurst that they should make their hedges sufficient between their tenements before the feast of the annunciation of the blessed Mary…'. This problem is mentioned again in 1583 'George and Oliver Harpyn and Thomas Wod have not made their doles and fences on the moor around the oats that have been sown there…therefore each is amerced (fined) of the lord…'. More references are seen in 1592 to 'not making doles' and not 'making up the gaps between the lands in their several tenures…'.

Collecting straw for bedding

An entry written on 4th November, 1550, reads 'Likewise they say that John Walker, Arthur Bynnes and William Marshe have dug and acquired the beddynge (straw bedding) on the common where they have no right…'.

Entertaining vagabonds

From 1558-1603 Elizabeth I reigned during a golden age of English history. In Tudor and Elizabethan times many people were wandering the country and looking for work, but with the rise in population during the sixteenth century work was often difficult to find. Some wandering beggars were disabled and the government tolerated these by giving them licences to beg. However, the government did not tolerate able-bodied people, who were without jobs, to wander around. They were seen as a threat to law and order; they were punished, whipped and forced to return to the parish in which they had been born or to where they had lived for the last three years. This practice can be seen at Farnley Tyas. In 1550 we read that 'An injunction has been made for Richard Grave and all others within the Demesne (land on a manor that was reserved for the lord's own use, as distinct from land held by the tenants) that in future they should not entertain vagabonds…'. This problem is mentioned again in 1601 'No …inhabitants of this manor shall entertain any persons called vagabonds or paupers from outside, nor shall they give any alms…'.

Stone-clearing the land

In 1550 on 4th November 'An injunction was made of John Wodd that from now on he should not gather stones on his own lands and throw them down on other people's lands…'.

Provision of coal

During the reign of Mary, in her attempts to restore England to Catholicism, her religious intolerance led to persecution of Protestants. But at this time fuel for their houses is an important subject for the Farnley Tyas tenants. On 30th December, 1557 tenants incurred fines because 'they had not provided for coals sufficiently to serve their houses for the whole year…'. In 1571 'An injunction was made that all persons shall provide and cart coals to serve their house according to the old custom…'. Likewise, on 3rd December, 1586 at the court of John Kaye held at Farnley Tyas 'John Kay of Royde House has not had enough coals and therefore is amerced (fined) of the Lord…'.

Managing the supply of water

During Elizabeth I's reign a yeoman clothier from Farnley Tyas called John Armytage married Elizabeth Kaye of Lockwood. He purchased the Kirklees estate in 1565 from Robert Pilkington and built a hall on the site of the old priory. Thus a farmer from Farnley Tyas became the earliest known member of the Armitage family to live at Kirklees Hall, near Brighouse. He died in 1574. However, the water supply was demanding attention in the village at Farnley Tyas.

'In 1560 at the court of Arthur Kaye held at Farnleytias on the 19th day of November in the third year of the reign of our lady Elizabeth an injunction was made that everyone should keep the watercourse scoured out in the intakkes (a duct or narrowing of a water channel) and not block out the said course nor turn it out of its old course'. In 1571, on 30th April, 'An injunction was made that no one shall wash sheep nor any things that are unwholesome in the well called the townewell'. In 1583 we read that 'A pain has been made that…no one shall wash wool within a distance of four yards of the common well…'. In 1592 'an agreement was made that everyone shall have the use of the common spring called the townewell…everyone for each bovate of land (as much land as an ox can plough in a year, usually estimated at fifteen acres) for the space of two days and so annually'.

Over use of the water supply was prohibited because others would be deprived of this valuable resource. In 1601 it was reported that 'George Harpyn senior has drained the water from Wigwell Well'. Again, in 1684 in the reign of Charles II, 'it is laid in paine that Thomas Mellor dreyne not the Towne Wells on paine of every time soe offending'.

Negotiating rights of way

In the days before road building the maintenance of established routes and rights of way was very important in a farming community, but these were sometimes contested in the community.

In 1563 'An injunction was made for Thomas Teilyour that in future he shall not plough a certain balk (an unploughed piece of land) at the Toftes but shall allow a way there to be used according to the old custom…'. This was an early example of the maintenance of a disputed right of way. Maintaining a right of way at the Croftes was alluded to in 1567 'An injunction was made that no one shall block the way over one headland over and through the Croftes on the south side of the township of Farnley…'. In 1603, in the reign of James I, England's first Stuart king, the same subject was recorded 'An injunction that John Firth shall permit his neighbours to pass with hay and corn over and across his close (a courtyard or enclosure) when the way in that same place is unsatisfactory…'. In 1603 we read 'Those who have need to use the way in the Cliff…should become contributors to the repairing and mending of the same whenever there is need'. In 1611, John Firth was again the subject of an injunction 'A lane called the Cliff Lane should be made by him adequate for carts before the first day of May…'.

Grinding corn and Woodsome Mill

There was an obligation, 'Suit of Mill,' for all tenants to resort to the lord's mill to have their corn ground. It was thus a profitable investment for the lord. The tenants also had to keep the water wheel in good repair; Farnley Tyas tenants would have ground their corn at Woodsome Mill.

In 1297 Nicholas de Farnley was recorded as lessee, from Sir Franco Teutonicus, for 20 years at 7s. 6d. per annum, of land at Farnley, with obligation to grind his corn at Wadehuse (Woodsome) Mill (*Dyson, T. 1951*).

In 1563 it was recorded in the Court Rolls that 'Thomas Beaumont and Robert Hurst have not made suit at the lord's mill with their corn…an injunction was made for Robert Hurst and all others that they should not withdraw from the lord's mill with their corn'. Another example of this control of corn milling can be seen in the Court Rolls of 1569 'An injunction was made for the freehold tenants within that (Farnley) manor that they shall show their evidence at the next court as to what milling they ought to render to the corn mill of the lord…'. The grinding of corn was a major aspect of everyday life which was, like so many features in the manorial system, under the control of the lord of the manor.

The tenant of Woodsome Mill in 1675 was John Crowther; earlier in the 1670s George and Thomas Bayldon held the tenancies. The Redfearn family entered into the tenancy of the mill and farm in 1678 and they held the tenancy from then onwards. Woodsome Mill is recorded in the 1828 Survey 'an old tenancy from the 1651 rental' and described as a stone and slate water corn mill containing four pairs of stones, two of which were kept going in 1828. In the 1838 Rate Book Richard Redfearn is listed as holding land, a corn mill and a house at Woodsome Mill for which he paid a rental of £39 14s. A later Richard Redfearn is listed in the 1923 Rate Book as being a tenant of the same property.

The mill was working up to 1932. Until the 1914-18 war Woodsome Mill was always very busy grinding corn and oats for the neighbouring farmers and for Sir John Ramsden after the mill on the Colne had ceased working. They used to make a lot of oatmeal and branmeal. This activity ceased after the war, from which time the mill ground oats for the immediate use of the farm (*Dyson, T.1951*).

Gathering turf for fires

The practice of cutting and carrying away gorse turf, used in fires, destroyed the lord's grass. In 1563 an injunction was made that 'No one shall carry away any turves gorse or any other things from his ploughed lands on the moor'. In 1603 the digging up of 'sods' or 'turves' was recorded at the court of Robert Kaye held at Farnley Tyas on 9th June. 'John Kaye of Roydhous…and William Tyas forfeited a pain …dug up sods (turves) at the dykeheads…three cartloads'. Also 'William Norcliffe has carried away sods from the moor without license of the lord, therefore he is amerced of the lord…'.

Archery

Archery is likely to have been a popular pastime in Farnley Tyas. The Assize of Arms of 1252 tells us that yeomen were required by law to practice archery and maintain their skills for military and hunting purposes (*www.livinghistory.co.uk/homepages/purbrook_bowman/statutes.htm*). Later, a statute of Henry VIII throws light on the importance of martial exercises at that time 'The Kyng, our Sovereign Lord, callynge to his most noble and most generous remembrance how by the feate and exercise of the subjecttes…in shooting in long bowes…good archers hath not only defended this realm…against the cruel malice and danger of their enemys…also have done many notable acts of warre against the infidels and others…'. The statute enacted that every man shall have a 'bowe and arrowe redy contynually in his house to use himself and do use himself in shotying…'.

He was also to 'teche and bring upp his children and servants in the knowledge of the same shotying'. 'Buttes were to be made in every citie, towne and place' and maintained at the common charge (*www.oxfordjournals.org/content*).

A record that archery was practised at Farnley Tyas can be seen in the manorial roll of 17th June, 1606 held at the court of Robert Kaye in Farnley Tyas. 'Richard Wode has carried off earth from the defined limits or goals used in archery (hath carried earth from the buttes), therefore he is amerced of the lord...'. Places where archery was practised were called 'butts'. Butts Road in Farnley Tyas still survives and it is likely that the butts used by the villagers were in this vicinity.

Fishing

Fishing is frequently mentioned in the manorial court roll, in the context of the breaching of regulations regarding where a tenant could fish. The consumption of fish was important in the medieval period and fishing would have been an essential way to find food in Farnley Tyas, but tenants could not fish without a licence from the lord.

'At the court of Arthur Kaye of Wodsom with Farnley Tyas on the last day of April in the thirteenth year of the reign of our Lady Elizabeth an injunction... (was made).. that no one shall fish in the stream between the demesne of Farnley and Thirsenland nor in the westwodd...'.In 1606 at the court of Robert Kaye held at Farnley Tyas on 17th June it was recorded that 'it has been made a pain that no one henceforth shall fish between James Brodehead yate (gate) and Little Wodsome.'. Also 'Richard Barbour and John Stables have fished in the stream on the demesne (the lord's land) where they had no right...'. Others 'fished without the licence of the lord...`and others 'fished with nets between Fenay Milne and Wodsome Milne where they have no right...'.

Hunting

Hunting without a licence was also an infringement of the lord's privileges. In 1684, in the reign of Charles II, it was stated 'that no person or persons doe hawke, hunt or course, shoote, fishe or any ways destroye the lord of the manor's game with any engine (gun) whatsoever without the lord's special licence...'.

Summary

The yeomen farmers of Farnley Tyas were subsistence farmers who made the most of the resources they needed but life must have been hard and harsh. Lives were controlled by the lords and by the farming year. Jean Froissart wrote in 1395 'the common people are bound by law and custom to plough the field of their masters, harvest the corn, gather it into barns and thresh and winnow the grain; they must also mow and carry home the hay, cut and collect wood and perform all manner of tasks of this kind...'. There were many duties to be performed in accordance with the tenant's lease or agreement. Money had to be paid in taxes or rent. A yeoman peasant had to pay rent for his land to his lord and he had to pay a tax to the church called a tithe. The manor was a dynamic agency in community affairs. It provided a bureaucracy and regulated a variety of complex activities. Led by the aristocracy, it depended on deferential behaviour from the yeomen tenants.

5. AGRICULTURE

Early records show that farming was, for a long period, the main occupation in Farnley Tyas. Several of the buildings in the village have seventeenth century date stones which are evidence of an active and prosperous farming community at this time. The oldest building in the village is a manor house barn, standing in Coronation Yard which is part of Yew Tree Farm. The barn has a date stone of 1673 (or possibly 1678), placing it in the period of the restored Stuart monarchy under Charles II. Nearby a date stone of 1678 can be seen on a farm cottage. At Park Farm, down Manor Road, there is the inscription "AGR 1693" on a barn. Yew Tree Farm has a date stone of 1692. This was a time of relative calm and prosperity after the after the beheading of Charles I in 1649 and the unpopular rule of Oliver Cromwell which ended in 1660. The dates reflect this and show a sense of achievement and pride on the part of the owners of the farms whose initials were often chiselled over the dates.

At times there were 30 farms in the village and in 1923 all these were in existence. Though dairy farming was the principle activity for many years, the last dairy farm ceased production in 2003; now (2015) none of the farms have dairy herds. In 2008 six of the farms were still working and three were tenanted - Beech Farm, Yew Tree Farm and Park House Farm. Low Common Farm is said to be one of the oldest farms in the area. Ivy Farm has been developed into an equestrian centre and at Sycamore Farm some of the redundant farm buildings have been converted into cottage holiday lets. Wood Farm has a diverse mix of activities (*Farnley Tyas Community Group 2008*). There is now just one working farm, Yew Tree Farm, specialising in beef cattle and still owned by the Farnley Estate. Most of the land on the Estate is now cultivated by contract farmers.

Medieval farming

It is the distinctive patterns in the fields which lie to the north-east of Farnley Tyas which give an indication of the early farming which took place in the area. The fields are called High Fields and Slate Fields and they are bisected by Field Lane. These were the medieval open fields of Farnley Tyas. In the middle ages this was arable land laid out in groups of strips shared among the Kayes' tenants, each group separated from the other by a balk or unploughed piece of land. These fields had no fences; they lay open and unenclosed.

Enclosure

During the sixteenth century this system of arable farming in open fields began to change: the process of enclosure redistributed the strips so that each man's lands were grouped together more conveniently and separated from the neighbour's by a fence or wall. The farming techniques, which had been used in England during feudal times, changed as the larger pieces of land made improved crop production possible. Some of the arable land gave way to grass, laying the foundation of the modern rural landscape. (*Redmonds, G. Huddersfield Examiner 2nd September, 1995*). We can read today in the manorial court rolls for 1563 an injunction saying that all tenants 'having doles (a share or portion of land) at Hyefield (High Field) shall make those same doles sufficient with walls ... every year one dole until the whole is finished'. Most of the local fences were thorn hedges which can still be seen today.

The land had been divided up in the strip cultivation system and each farm had been allocated land that was potentially good and also land that was of poor quality; thus on each farm land was scattered. Manor Farm (opposite the Golden Cock) had land at the bottom of Field Lane and at Farnley Hey. This was a distance of one and a half miles and must have been uneconomic. The agents Carter Jonas who took over management of the Estate in 1956 negotiated exchanges of land with tenants, reduced the number of farms and consolidated the holdings into viable units (*Beaumont, D.M. 1985*).

Manor house barn (1673) in Coronation Yard in 1954
(Courtesy Huddersfield Examiner,)

A present-day view of Slate Fields and High Fields showing enclosure.

Farnley Moor

The clearing of Farnley Moor for agricultural use had been progressing since the latter half of the sixteenth century when 'John Kay cleared the Moor for agriculture, marled and limed it...' (*Beaumont. D.M.1985.p.28*). Evidently the whole of the Moor was not cleared then; Dartmouth Estate records (*Kirklees Archives*) for 1772 show that enclosing and cultivating Farnley Moor was continuing and was actively encouraged and supported by Lord Dartmouth whose agent wrote 'The two sons of William Slaytor to have twenty-five pounds each at interest to build houses upon Farnley Moor, each to inclose at his own expense two or three acres off the Moor...' and 'Bill Wood to have something allowed him towards the expenses of walling upon Farnley Moor...'. In 1773 'William Wood is to have a little money for his house...but my Lord will assist him a little in his new inclosure on Farnley Moor...'. When Lord Dartmouth's agents, Kent, Pearce and Kent, were reporting in the early nineteenth century they were also taking steps to bring the waste into cultivation. In the 1805 Survey (*Dartmouth Estate 1805 p.118*) there is a reference to Joseph Scafe's 'new enclosed moorland...fences not yet completed' and 'James Slater...on Farnley Moor...2 closes to be inclosed...'.

In 1808 the Agents instructed that 'Notices should be given to Jonas Kaye to take in a piece of waste next to the moor at Farnley Bank; the like to George Eastwood...also one to B. Hirst to cultivate the piece of moorland...unless they did so I would take their land away'. 'Reserved rents' in the 1805 Survey were an acknowledgement to people 'who have built themselves dwellings etc. on the waste and likewise for such of the waste whereon they fix tenters...' (*p.148*). It seems that the existing tenants could not cope with all the waste lands. The enclosure of these therefore provided work for the poor. In the rental of 1818 there are shown a number of increases varying from 2s. 6d. to £1 5s., the explanatory remarks being 'New rent from Lammas (1st August) 1817, for land cleared by the Poor in the Winter 1816/17' (*Beaumont, D.M. 1985 p.28*).

Tithes

Originally tithes were payments in kind (crops, wool, milk etc.) consisting of an agreed proportion of the yearly profits from farming and made by parishioners for the support of their parish church and its clergy (*www.nationalarchives.gov.uk/records/research-guides/tithe-records*). Tithes were divided into great and small tithes; generally corn, grain, hay and wood were considered to be great tithes, payable to the rector or land owner, others were classed as small tithes, often paid to the vicar of the parish. During the dissolution of the monasteries much church land and the accompanying tithes passed into lay ownership. Frequently a vicar continued to have spiritual oversight of the parish and so continued to receive small tithes. From early times money payments began to be substituted for payments in kind. In 1836 tithes were still payable in most parishes; the Tithe Commutation Acts were passed in that year. The principle was to substitute the payment of tithes in kind to 'corn rent' or a 'tithe rent charge'. This was not subject to local variation but was calculated on an average for the whole country.

In the early nineteenth century the tenant farmers at Farnley Tyas would have been paying a tithe to the church (or the Vicar of Almondbury) in kind. In the 1805 Survey (*Dartmouth Estate 1805 p.5*) we read 'Farnley and Honley are in Almondbury Parish and are free of great tithes but subject to small tithes'. The tithes had not yet been 'commuted' and so were payable in kind; a proportion of the produce from the crops grown on the land. It was however, customary to accept cash payment in lieu. The collection of the tithe from each individual grower, before the crop was disposed of, was impracticable so the tithes were therefore changed to an agreed rent (*Beaumont D.M. 1985*). The tithe was not fully converted to a monetary value in Farnley Tyas until 1847.

The Farnley Tyas tithe award and map of 1847 shows the 'Apportionement of the rent charge in lieu of tithes in the township of Farnley Tyas in the Parish of Almondbury in the West Riding of the County of York'. This was drawn up on 18th November, 1847 and was confirmed by the Tithe Commissioners for England and Wales. Its purpose was to 'Award the sums to be paid by way of Rent charge instead of the Tithes of the Township of Farnley Tyas...'. Meetings were held and due notice was given. The overseer and Barrister at Law was John Job Rawlinson of Graythwaite in the County of Lancaster. His job as an Assistant Tithe Commissioner was to award the sums to be paid by way of rent charge instead of the tithes of the township of Farnley Tyas.

It seems that the great tithes were already being paid in money 'I find that there is an ancient and laudable custom that all the occupiers... of land in the Township should pay to the Impropriation of the Tithes (the destination of the income from tithes, from the church to a layman)...at the Feast of St. Michael the Archangel the sum of Ten pence halfpenny instead of all the great tithes of the said Township...'.

John Rawlinson recorded that 'instead of the tithes of milk and calves in kind the custom is that every occupier of land...who has had fewer than five calves within the year should pay three halfpence for every such calf...the same custom is observed in tithing geese, pigs and lambs...a half penny is payable for every goose, pig or lamb under five...'. These would have been small tithes, payable to the Vicar of Almondbury.

The Assistant Tithe Commissioner found that all the lands in Farnley Tyas were subject to payment 'of all manner of Tithes in kind except as aforesaid' (already mentioned). In his Award he declared that the Governors of Clitheroe Grammar School were the impropriators of all the great tithes and the Vicar of Almondbury was entitled to all the small tithes. The Award granted the sum of 'Ten pence half penny by way of rent charge to the Governors of Clitheroe Grammar School...instead of all the great tithes...and the annual sum of twenty-five pounds, also by way of rent charge, should be paid to the Vicar for the time being...instead of all the small tithes...'.The rent charges were to be in lieu 'not only of all tithes payable in kind but also in lieu of all customary payments for tithes...'.

This more efficient and 'modernized' system of rent collection must have made a considerable difference to the Farnley tenants. Canon Hulbert, (*Hulbert, C. A. 1880 p.76*) wrote that the Reverend Lewis Jones 'had a vast amount of trouble and difficulty in collecting the Tithes...under the old law...and among the important works which he achieved was the Commutation into a Rent Charge of all the Tithes of the thirteen Townships in the Parish. Easter dues, Mortuaries etc. were all Commuted into a Rent Charge...'.

The tithe rent charge was collected by Lord Dartmouth by way of extra rent from the tenants. In the Account Book of 1864 most of the tenants on the Farnley Tyas estates had their 'rent increased from Lammas 1863 for Land Tax and Tithe Rent Charge' (*Beaumont, D.M. 1985 p. 40*).

The Farnley Industrial Field

A noteworthy feature of agriculture at Farnley Tyas in the middle of the nineteenth century was the Farnley Industrial Field. This was an interesting experiment which had its origins both in the encouragement of good husbandry and a theory that 'unskilled labour applied to the land, by the spade, will, under common sense management return its value' (*Huddersfield Chronicle 30th November, 1850*).

The Farnley Tyas industrial farm was of great importance in the village and made a unique contribution to agricultural development in the area. The cultivation of the soil was pre-eminent. This preoccupation was manifested in the Spade Husbandry and Stall Feeding Association which was promoted by the Earl of Dartmouth at the suggestion of his agent Frederick Thynne of Westminster. John Nowell was an enthusiastic and tireless worker for this cause. Hulbert (*p.179*) explains the origins of the activity: it was 'as a remedy for frequent depressions in trade, and the comparative neglect of the cultivation of the land; from which much benefit resulted: waste lands were broken up, relief given by labour, new roads made, and cottage gardening promoted'. The 1840s and 1850s were a time of depression and hardship for the Farnley people, some of whom depended on trade for their livelihood. Some cottagers had no land.

A report of the The Woodsome Hall Spade Husbandry Festival shows the support of the movement given by Lord Dartmouth and also demonstrates that it generated considerable social activity. 'The committees of the Spade Husbandry Associations on the estates of the Earl of Dartmouth at Farnley Tyas and Slaithwaite and other friends of the same cause from the surrounding villages…were entertained on the seventh annual occasion most hospitably in the ancient mansion of the Kayes and Legges (Woodsome Hall). Frederick Thynne presided. At four o'clock the company sat down in the fine old Elizabethan hall to an excellent dinner provided, at his lordship's expense, by Mr. Kaye of Farnley. The Rev. Cutfield Wardroper attended, as did the Rev. C. A. Hulbert. The evening closed at 8 o'clock and the spirit was described as one of 'hilarity and good feeling' (*Huddersfield Chronicle 19th June, 1852*).

However, more background information regarding the benefits of this very energetic movement was outlined in the speeches. It was seen as 'beneficial for the reduction of parochial rates by employing paupers in reproductive labour, for the education of the young in parochial agriculture, as well as affording an agreeable and healthy recreation to masters and scholars, and as tending to raise the character and circumstances of cottagers'. The organisers planned to prepare for a period of manufacturing distress by having some work of spade labour ready. The employment provided by Spade Husbandry Societies was 'expected to prepare labourers for usefulness at home on our own waste lands, or abroad'.

An early meeting of the Central Committee of Farnley Tyas Industrial Farm, held on 30th November, 1850 and reported in the *Huddersfield Chronicle* gives more details of the running of the farms. The Committee possessed a small farm of four and a half acres of moorland which had been cultivated for a year by spade labour. A donation from the Manufacturers' Relief Committee had been given in 1842 '

> *not wishing at that time to fritter it away in road-side stone-breaking, and thus to degrade decent working men into paupers, the money was laid out, with a view to its reproduction, in a field taken for a term of four years. For four successive years, by careful management, this grant of £40.00 was found to reproduce itself, through growing crops raised by spade cultivation'.*

It provided employment for poor men for 800 days, at certain periods. The land had not been used since 1846 but in 1850 it was once more called into action. In spite of the Farnley Moor soil being impoverished and worn out the first year's crop showed a gratifying result. An accurate account of all expenses was kept and at the end of the first

17

year the money realised on the produce was greater than the outlay. The money thus given back by the ground during the first year was made use of in payment of wages for work done in the same ground for the relief of the same men during the second year. During the remaining two years of the tenancy this money was twice put into the ground in the shape of unskilled labour and twice was faithfully restored. The Committee expected that their fund would remain as a permanent fund and 'prevent to some extent the unemployed from being a burden to the parish officer'.

In 1850 a small farm on Farnley moor was taken on a permanent tenancy. An article in the *Huddersfield Chronicle* 4th December, 1852 gives us a picture of the hardships of life for the unemployed in Farnley Tyas at this time 'to this farm, as a last resort, men repair to get a little wholesome work when they have nothing else to do...applicants for parish relief are also there...the work is generally labour with the spade, fork or hoe, instruments very easily wielded, and it is chiefly let by the piece at fair prices...and persons are here who could tell what a benefit employment there has been to them'. Cornelius Kaye, assistant overseer, managed the farm and its success was due to his good husbandry. The population of Farnley Tyas was 800 in 1852 and it was conjectured that with a forty or fifty acre farm, adequate capital and a careful, experienced manager like Mr. Kaye the dependent poor might be supported with very small, possibly without any, aid from the poor rate.

The Farnley Central Committee shared the philanthropic motives for the promotion of the industrial farm and in the report in the *Huddersfield Chronicle* 4th December, 1852 the purpose of the Farm is put in its national context 'poor-law authorities, guardians of the poor and the 'poor-law association", supported by noblemen and gentlemen of every political party are beginning to call public attention to the devising of methods for setting the poor to work and in various unions of England and Ireland this is in part already accomplished: it is to be hoped that the efforts here...will prove a valuable contribution to the cause'. It seems that Farnley was a forerunner in these endeavours 'many enquiries from distant friends' had been received. The example set by Farnley Tyas did inspire the villagers of Penn in Buckinghamshire to start a similar scheme but sadly we do not know how successful this was. 'Certainly there was no general adoption of the plan...'. (*Redmonds, G. Huddersfield Examiner 17th July, 1982*) However, in their own village, the Farnley Tyas people did help the community by creating meaningful employment for able-bodied men who otherwise would have sought poor relief at the workhouse.

Allotment gardens

These were seen as a thriving addition to farming in the village and their cultivation made the inhabitants renowned. In the *Huddersfield Chronicle* 6th December, 1851 the Rev. Lewis Jones reported that 'it was gratifying to find that the example which the inhabitants of Farnley Tyas had set before the country during the last 10 years had been followed by very many persons in different parts of the country'. In the parish of Farnley Tyas there were 'upwards of a thousand field allotments'. Crops were oats, turnips, wheat and potatoes. On 27th August at the Farnley Tyas Spade Husbandry Association the Rev. Cutfield Wardroper expressed the wish that 'not only in this township but throughout the length and breadth of the land every cottager might have his plot of ground' (*Huddersfield Chronicle 21st June, 1851*). At the Spade Husbandry Festival at Woodsome Hall the 'prosperous condition of allotment gardens' was mentioned. But the dichotomy between industrialisation and agriculture was being felt: the prosperity on the land was in spite of manufacturing prosperity which 'drew men's minds...from the pursuits of agriculture'. However, a scientific approach to agriculture was in evidence 'some experiments had been made with substances...into the composition of manure...'. In the future similar experiments were desirable.

6. THE DARTMOUTH ESTATE

With the exception of a very small number of privately owned properties the whole of Farnley Tyas, and much of the area surrounding it, was once part of the Earl of Dartmouth's estate which was administered from the Manor House in Slaithwaite. This office has now closed, though it is still owned by Lord Dartmouth, and the intention is to alter its use from office to residential. Dartmouth Estate documents have been transferred to archive centres in Leeds and Kirklees but some old records are with Carter Jonas in their Harrogate office and are used as working documents.

Lord Dartmouth's Yorkshire Estates originally included Farnley Tyas, part of Thurstonland, Brockholes, Honley, Meltham, Almondbury, Lepton, Kirkburton, Slaithwaite and Morley. Now (2015) it includes 4,000 acres in Slaithwaite and just under 1,000 acres in Morley where much of the land has been sold for development. There is still some land on Honley Moor and one farm in Lepton which are under Dartmouth ownership. These are managed by Carter Jonas from offices in York, Harrogate and Leeds.

In 1968, the ninth Earl, Gerald, sold the whole of the 2,000 acre Farnley Estate (the land and property which was not already in private hands) to a local family. This land has since been known as Farnley Estates. The Earl died in 1973 and his son, the tenth Earl, William, is now the owner of the Dartmouth Estate. The family used to live at Patshull in Staffordshire; the large house and forestry land have now been sold to the local authority and the current Earl, who is a Member of the European Parliament, owns a house in London and an estate in Devon (*David Pedley in conversation*).

The agents

The third Earl of Dartmouth succeeded to the title in 1801 and became dissatisfied with the management of his Yorkshire estates. He dismissed the agent William Emsall, whose family had managed the Estate since it had come into Dartmouth ownership, and appointed Kent, Pearce and Kent as his London agents. By 1855 the name of the firm had changed to Thynne and Thynne. Mr Eagland was the resident agent under Thynne and Thynne and the Estate remained under their management until 1955/56 when Lord Dartmouth offered the management of the Estate to Carter Jonas. Dorothy Beaumont then ran the Estate, from Slaithwaite, for two years after which time, in 1958, Carter Jonas appointed John Patterson as their agent. He modernised a house down Manor Road and lived in the village. When John Patterson retired in 1964 David Pedley became the agent for the Dartmouth Estate until the Farnley Estate part was sold in 1968; David Pedley continued to work for Carter Jonas until his retirement.

Local stewards were appointed to run the estates; in 1804 the steward at Farnley Tyas was Jonathan Senior who had overall responsibility for Lord Dartmouth's Yorkshire estates. He was succeeded by his son. In 1858 Gilbert Wilson had an appointment 'care of the woods and game' and he eventually took over all the duties of Bailiff and occupied the Bailiff's (Gamekeeper's) cottage near the Hall. He was followed by his son, Joseph G. Wilson, who died in 1916.

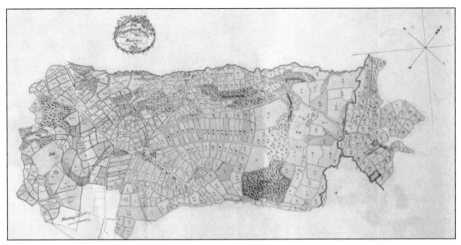

1805 Terrier of the Dartmouth Estate (Courtesy Farnley Estates)

The 1805 Survey of the Dartmouth Estate

After Kent, Pearce and Kent had been appointed in 1804 immediate steps were taken to increase the rents on the three Yorkshire estates (Slaithwaite, Farnley Tyas and Morley). Pearce wrote: …'nothing harsh is intended to be done towards them (the tenants), that all their rents will be viewed and a fair rent put on them…and that they will have the first offer…where buildings have been done by the tenants a due consideration will be paid to that circumstance…we wish them not to be alarmed at the measure…that it is only a new arrangement of the Rental that is intended…' (*Beaumont, D. M. 1985 p.8*).

Mr. W. Pearce stayed at the George Inn in Huddersfield from 22nd September until 18th October, 1804. This was apparently to hold the Rent Audits (collection of rents), but he wrote to Jonathan Senior on 4th September 'I intend looking at each tenant's holdings…so as to be able to offer them their respective Tenements at a fresh rent on those days…'. On 10th October he wrote to Lord Dartmouth 'The tenants at Farnley have all agreed with me with the exception of Mr. Scott who has requested time to decide. I must confess that I am sorry that he should be so singular. It is fortunate that the other tenants are not led by his example however…"(*Beaumont, D. M. 1985 p.8*).

Thus, in 1805 Lord Dartmouth's agents Kent, Pearce and Kent completed a rent revision for the Yorkshire Estates. They then considered it advisable to prepare 'a register' giving detailed information of the whole of the Estates. In a letter to Lord Dartmouth Mr. Pearce said that it 'shows the present disposition of the property'. In this Survey of 1805 (*Dartmouth Estate 1805*) each holding is dealt with separately, giving the name of the building or farm, the name of the tenant, the name of each field and its number on the key map, its type of cultivation, i.e. meadow, pasture or arable, the rents before and after the increase and the buildings on the holding. The mills and collieries are listed with detailed information on each. The script is in a beautiful copperplate hand and there are delightful illustrations. Apart from the value of the information it contains, the book itself is a work of art.

A most interesting aspect of the Estate Survey is the light which it throws on the way in which Lord Dartmouth and his tenants jointly financed the improvements of both farming and commercial premises. If tenants advanced money themselves for rebuilding, conversion or extension of premises, a lease was often granted at an artificially low 'reserved rent' which acted as an incentive for such improvements (*Hudson, P.1975*). This can be seen at Farnley Mill where the 'reserved rent' was £5 0s 0d as recorded in the 1805 survey.

Other examples of this goodwill which can be seen in the Survey are:

1. *at Runnett End William Harping paid a rent of £13 10s for a house and shop. Lord Dartmouth had 'advanced money for buildings'.*
2. *also at Runnett End Joseph Harping had 'a house, shop and laithe' which had been built by Lord Dartmouth.*
3. *again at Runnett End John Hepworth had 'a good house and barn' for which '£30 0s 0d (had been) originally loaned by Lord Dartmouth".*
4. *at Littlewoods Barnabas Hirst had 'a house and a barn' and he 'had £40 0s 0d of Lord Dartmouth".*
5. *in Brockholes Mrs. Jagger 'had a range of buildings used as tenements and Lord Dartmouth had advanced £20 0s 0d".*
6. *at Top of Town, the Wood, John, Charles, and George Shaw are described as ' being poor people, holding their tenements at rack rents, no alteration was made in their rent'.*

Hudson states that 'Lord Dartmouth was a rare example in the West Riding of a prominent, active, improving landlord' (*p. 89*).

In addition to the Mill and other premises in Farnley Tyas Lord Dartmouth also owned and leased smaller clothiers' dwellings and farmsteads. The 1805 Survey states that he owned six groups of clothiers' premises in the village, leased at a rent of £128 10s.

The Survey also gives valuable information about the holdings and occupations of the villagers in 1805.

At Ludwell, William Bradley had 'a new house, a barn, a shop and a dye house'. Detailed accounts are given of the buildings at each holding. At Netherton Jon Eastwood had 'a house' and 'other buildings and a cottage...'. At Town George Eastwood had a 'farm house and other out buildings...'. At Farnley Bank William Hallas had 'a good dwelling house and two cottages with outbuildings, house shop and laithe...'. Many of the holdings included a laithe which was a barn combining a cow-house with crop storage space. At Littlewoods William Jagger had 'a house, laithe and outbuildings...'. William Nowels had a 'farmhouse, new barn, outhouse...' at Birks and William Roberts also had a 'good house and several outbuildings' at Birks.

John Schofield had a farmhouse with several outbuildings and a saddlers shop and a range of tenements at Ludwell.

Joseph Smith was a butcher; he had a 'house, butcher's shop and outhouses'.

Tanning

Tanning is the process of treating animal skins to produce leather. Tannin, which came from oak or fir trees, was traditionally used to make the leather. The skins would first be soaked in water to clean and soften them so a tan yard would always have pits for this purpose. We see from the 1805 Survey that there were several tanneries in the village; they also can be identified on the map of 1854.

At Sycamore, where the tenants were Charles and Jonas Kaye, there was 'a house and out buildings and a tan house and a yard...'. Later, in 1838, the Rate Book records that Joseph and John Kaye had land and buildings, also a 'hous and tanyard' at Sycamore. At Roydhouse, where the tenant in 1805 was Sarah Kaye, there was a 'farmhouse, barn,

Tan house and pump at the bottom of Manor Road, 1980. (Courtesy Farnley Estates)

Mr. J. Shaw samples spring water from Woodland View at the bottom of Manor Road. The spring used to feed the pits of a tanyard where the tanning of leather was carried out. The tanyard pits still existed in 1954

(Courtesy Huddersfield Examiner).

Tan pit, 1954
(Courtesy Farnley Estates)

outhouses, tan house and yard...'. Also at Roydhouse Thomas Kaye had a 'farmhouse, laithe and tanyard...'. In 1838 Jonathan Roberts was tenant of a house, land, buildings and a tanyard as recorded in the Rate Book. Yet another tannery was at the edge of the village, in the fields at the top of the Woodsome Road, just below the site of the Wesleyan Church which was built much later. The tanning operation did sometimes cause annoyance to those who were living in the vicinity as is seen from a note in the Farnley Tyas Local Board Minute Book for 1888: 'The clerk was instructed to give notice to Messrs. Kaye and Son that they were causing a nuisance injurious to health by boiling flesh etc. at the Tanyard with their apparatus in its present inefficient state...if it occurs again proceedings will be initiated against them without further notice...'.

Collieries

An early record of coal mining can be seen in the Dartmouth Estate books. The Yorkshire Rental for 1651, when the Estate was owned by the Kayes, shows mines between Shaw Head and Woodroyd, Honley.

Most of Farnley Tyas coal came from Brockholes where the tenant in 1805 was Joseph Haigh. Beaumont (1985) reports that in 1805 there was an increased demand for coal and the higher prices encouraged prospectors to open up new collieries and seams. In 1810 Joseph Haigh opened up another seam in Brockholes and he is listed in the 1838 Rate Book as being the tenant of a colliery at Westwood, also of a saw mill and a blacksmith's shop.

The 1805 Survey states that new terms were made with the colliers; it was stipulated that they should sell a certain measure for a certain price. Previous to this the public had been 'grossly imposed upon...' having to put up with short measures and varying prices. Lord Dartmouth's agents also had to achieve a fair rent for the Lord's share of the mine.

There was another seam, of 18 ins., at Westwood which was in a poor state of production. The tenant was Widow Jagger. Lord Dartmouth's agents described the sad state of affairs 'the mine has been worked in an improper way for many years...is nothing like so productive as Joseph Haigh's, although the collieries are very near each other. The present tenant has been imposed on by the Colliers and the Works very ill managed, so that the mine cannot at times be worked on account of water in it. She is, however, desirous of continuing Tenant, although I feel it will never answer to her...'. She must have been a difficult tenant; in 1806 Mr. Pearce wrote 'as usual she was full of complaints at her losses...' (Beaumont, D.M. 1985 p. 30).

The last colliery to be worked at Farnley Tyas was the Woodsome colliery at Fenay Bridge by Lockwood and Elliott, trading as Huddersfield Collieries Ltd. They stopped working around 1939 and had an auction sale of all the effects in the early 1940s.

Stone quarries

A study of the map of 1854 shows several quarries in close proximity to Farnley Tyas. There is documentary evidence on maps and in entries in Local Board Minute Books of numerous small stone quarries on the Estate; their remains can still be seen in the landscape.

Most of the cottages in the village were built in local stone from these quarries, enabling them to be built at a low cost. The tenants themselves would have got the stone from the quarries. During the nineteenth century stone would have been needed for road making, walls, drains, houses, farm buildings, roof slates and flagstone for floors. The Local

Government Board for the Township of Farnley Tyas met in the national schoolroom and the Minute Books report regular requests for stone from the Surveyor; several quarries are mentioned. For example: in 1887 'The Surveyor reported that he required 16 tons of broken stones to complete New Lane Top and towards Town End...the Clerk was empowered to order...'. 'The Surveyor further reported that he required 350 yards of stone for Haley Croft Top and Butts and 100 yards in New Line Quarry for Rushfield... he was instructed to get this...'. At each of the monthly meetings the amount spent on repairs of the Highways was reported. Other quarries mentioned are Stone Stack, Burnt Slack and Cliff Quarry 'The surveyor reported that he would have some of this stone'. He was instructed to take some – there must have been disputes over the rights which people had to take stone from quarries. In September 1888 there was a discussion 'over what authority the surveyor had to allow John Heywood to get stone in (the) quarry adjoining Nowell's wood. He explained that this would have been broken up into road stone...Heywood thought it was worth something better...Heywood was asked to pay...'. Notes in the Minute Books show the increasing demand for stone 'The footpath at Butts should be edged with stone...'. A wall needed to be repaired 'for the safety of foot passengers...'. It was agreed to purchase 'road stone chippings...'. Inevitably there were difficulties 'Mr. Joe Capper was ordered not to take any more land from any of the roads without the sanction of the surveyor...'. The 1923 Rate Book states that W.A. Kaye and others owned a quarry occupied by Farnley Tyas Urban District Council. The rental was £3. 0s. and the rates were 14s. 0d..

Woodlands

The planting, thinning, fencing and general upkeep of woodlands was an important part of Dartmouth Estate management. Notes about woodland management were recorded in the Agents Letter and Memoranda Book 1804-1810. The third Earl of Dartmouth, who succeeded to the title in 1801, and who had appointed the agents Kent, Pearce and Kent in 1805, required them to plant 'further plantations at 10 acres per year...'. The half moon plantations which can still be seen up Field Lane followed on this instruction (*Beaumont, D. M. 1985 p.34*).

Under the heading 'Thinning of plantations' there is a note from the agent in the Letter Book 'Reminded Jonathan (the steward) that I wish the thinning of plantations to be about £150 every year – very little more or less. Also to plant 1 or 2000 ash 2 feet in the last Fall in the Carr – and also to fill up the Slang at the top of Farnley Mills dams".

On a Farnley visit on 28th October, 1807, the agent wrote:

Viewed the Brooke that is cut straight by Hepworth and approved of the same. It will want walling and that will cost £5. Told Jonathan to aquaint Hepworth that I would be £2.10.0 towards the improvement. Viewed Mollicarr Wood wherein there is four large trees – told Jonathan not to cut all the large trees here. NB This wood comes down the ensuing winter...NB There is a dead ash tree by Royd House about 40 ft that is to be fallen and brought into Jonathan Senior's thinning account. Also another by Farnley Mill about 40ft'. In May 1810 Jonathan Senior was instructed to: 'Plant 8 or 10 oaks and beech in the copse at Woodsome and thin the young larch plantations in order to give room to the oaks and forest trees...

In the autumn of 1810 he was instructed to 'Plant Hunters Nab about 1 acre with larch, beech and sycamore. Also plant about one and a half acres of Kaye's Close below the Upper Tan Yard...trees should be planted: ash, oak, sycamore, poplar and a few larch...'.

Sometimes trees were chopped down unlawfully and this unauthorised chopping was dealt with harshly. In October 1809 the agents recorded that 'Two of Scott's men, having been fined by the Magistrates 40s each for cutting hazels in Carr Wood – gave the £4 this day to the Poor of Farnley to celebrate the Jubilee…'. (George III's golden jubilee was on 25th October, 1809).

The 1828 Survey of the Dartmouth Estate

This Survey does not vary a great deal from the 1805 Survey but it does show an increase in the size of the holdings and a greater range of activities in which the tenants were involved (*Beaumont, D. M. 1985*).

In the village there were 24 farmhouses with farm buildings and 36 cottages, a blacksmith's shop, a butcher's shop and the public house, the Golden Cock (*Beaumont, D. M. 1985 p.28*). In addition to their farming activities a number of tenants were also engaged in trade.

Richard Roberts had a house of 14 rooms, barn, stable, cowhouse, cropping shop and chamber. George Shaw had a house, buildings and dyehouse; John Roberts had a house, barn stable, cowhouse, cartshed, a drying room, leather shop and large cattle shed. Mr Roberts still had the premises in 1845 but he wrote to Lord Dartmouth's agent, Mr. C.F. Thynne, who in turn wrote to Lord Dartmouth in March of that year 'I find a letter here from Mr. Roberts, the tanner of Farnley, who from continued ill health is about giving up that business and planting his son on the premises as a brewer and converting them into a Brewery for which, from the supply of water, they are very well adapted'. Lord Dartmouth consented to this conversion and the premises were known for many years as 'the old brewery'. Mr. William Nowell of The Wood had a house of six rooms, farm buildings, a house of three rooms used as a wool warehouse, a large warehouse, dyehouse and shop. James and George Sykes of Hunter's Nab had a house, two cottages, buildings and a dyehouse built in 1824. At Roydhouse there was a tan yard in the occupation of John Kay who, in addition to his house and farm buildings had a mill, cartshed and half a building used as a leather shop. Joseph Leigh of Roydhouse had the other half of the building, also used as a leather shop. Redfearn of Woodsome Mill had a corn mill (*Beaumont, D.M. 1985 p.29*).

Social life and Woodsome Hall

Farnley Tyas residents must have enjoyed the social life which their proximity to Woodsome Hall gave them; there are numerous records of social activities at the Hall in which Farnley residents would have taken a part.

The Dartmouths had greater estates in Staffordshire and so did not always live at Woodsome Hall; agents managed the estates and tenants occupied the Hall. However, in 1842 the Hall was occupied by the Earl's land agent and for several years the Rev. Cutfield Wardroper lived at the Hall before the Parsonage was built. Eventually however the Dartmouth's personal supervision was restored with their residence at Woodsome from time to time. In the 1850s the fifth Earl, William Walter, took up residence at Woodsome and the Hall was refurbished. It was used for shooting parties and the Game Book shows evidence of good seasons. Carr Wood and the surrounding Farnley estate provided good sport (*Holroyd, A. 1993 p.2*).

The 1838 Rate Book shows that the Keeper's Cottage was empty in that year but after that it was in use; Mr. Gilbert Wilson looked after the game and lived at Keeper's Cottage rent free. On 23rd April and 14th May, 1864 it was reported in the *Huddersfield Chronicle* that the noble Earl authorised Gilbert Wilson to kill game on the estate and distribute it to tenants, especially to poor and sick families. 182 families benefitted on the Farnley estate. The tenant farmers were pleased because their crops were saved from destruction and

Farnley Shoot c 1900 left to right: Jimmy Roberts (Farnley Brewery), Henry Sykes, anon', John Shaw, Joseph Wilson, Birkett with three dogs.

Farnley Shoot c.1900 left to right: Mark Shaw, David Beldon and Willie Shaw with three dogs (both courtesy Farnley Estates)

the poor were pleased because their difficulties were relieved. Over a period of six years 2,000 head of game were distributed in the Dartmouth estate and poaching became almost unknown. Rabbits were numerous on parts of the Farnley estate; farmers complained to Gilbert Wilson 'about rabbits doing damage to their crops near the Moor'. However, 'no expense of labour had been spared to utterly destroy them' and Gilbert Wilson reported in 1864 that very few were on the estate. He said that if the tenants had a poor crop of wheat it was from causes other than the game.

There was much excitement in September 1856 when the fifth Earl of Dartmouth and the Countess visited Woodsome. It was reported that they 'displayed much affability, kindness and consideration to all...'. The Farnley Tyas people appreciated this so much that an address, signed by the tenantry of the village, was presented in front of the Hall ' amidst a numerous assemblage of the inhabitants generally, including the scholars and teachers of Farnley Tyas and Almondbury schools,...the Reverend Cutfield Wardroper, the incumbent of Farnley Tyas...read the address...'. He read that 'We, the tenantry within...the district of Farnley Tyas...beg leave most respectfully to address your Lordship and your Countess...'. Lord Dartmouth replied in the same vein. He rejoiced at the opportunity of meeting his tenants again and thanked them for the kind feelings they had shown. He hoped that in future he and the Countess would be able to make frequent visits to the Woodsome and Farnley Tyas area. When he was absent he felt that he was well represented by Mr. Thynne (his agent) who was much respected by them. The relationship between a Lord and his tenants in the nineteenth century is clearly expressed 'Mr. Thynne...faithfully made known to him the feelings and wishes of his tenants...'. He was 'always glad to receive any application...reserving always to himself the right to refuse it if he saw good reason for doing so, after giving the application his best consideration' (*Beaumont,D. M. 1985 p.46*).

Farnley residents must have been delighted when three of William Walter's daughters, Frances, Georgina and Elizabeth, came to live at the Hall; they took much interest in the welfare of Farnley tenants (*Beaumont, D.M. 1985 p. 43*). After the death of William

Gamekeeper's
cottage near
Woodsome Hall

27

Programme for an afternoon festivity at Woodsome in 1907
(Olde English Village Faire. Woodsome. 1907)

1906 Ordnance Survey map of Farnley Tyas
(Courtesy Huddersfield Local Studies Library)

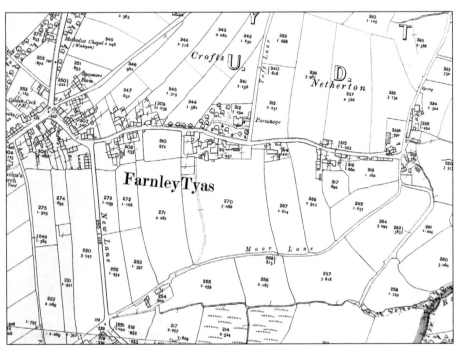

Walter in 1891 the Hall was used as a Dower house for the Countess and her daughters; the village benefitted from their presence. Lord Dartmouth had built a reading room for the young men of the village; the single storey, two roomed building is still there in the centre of the village, at the bend in the road. It was the headquarters of the Home Guard during World War II and was used as a 'radio listening centre'. In 1988 it was converted into a small house. The sisters wanted to help the women of the village so they set up the 'Mothers' Home' which was a large wooden hut where the ladies could meet for social functions, sewing etc. It was built on land down Manor Road, near the top at the right hand side, which was lent rent free to the caretaker. During World War II it was used for whist drives, social evenings and money raising efforts for the war. After the war it was sold but some villagers still remember going to dances there.

The Dartmouth ladies were leaders in religious and social activities in the village during Victorian and Edwardian days. Photos recall garden parties and fancy dress and festive occasions at Woodsome Hall. Photographs and programmes show garden parties, concerts, plays, Morris dancing, maypole dancing, wrestling, crowning of the May Queen, olde English sports, country dancing and other festive occasions at Woodsome Hall. (*Cocker, K. M. in Mallinson, C. H. and Warwick, G. M. eds. 1990*).

In 1902 there was a grand celebration on the occasion of the twenty-first birthday of the sixth earl's eldest son. He became the seventh earl in 1936 but in 1902 he celebrated in grand style at Woodsome Hall; all the tenants on the Yorkshire estates were invited and brought by special train from Slaithwaite and Morley to the station at Fenay Bridge. Lord Dartmouth wrote a pageant in verse for the occasion which was performed by the young people of Farnley Tyas on the terrace in front of the Hall. Further pageants, hosted by the three Dartmouth ladies and attended by Farnley tenants, were apparently a great success. The ladies left Woodsome in 1910 and were much missed by the people of Farnley (*Holroyd, A. 1993 p. 4*).

The sixth Earl of Dartmouth continued the tradition of benevolence to the village: in 1927 he gave land, on Butts Road, of nearly five acres to Thurstonland and Farnley Tyas Urban District Council. There is a plaque on the wall near the entrance to the recreation ground which states that it was 'to be used as a public pleasure ground and for the purposes of cricket, football or other games or recreations, or as the site of buildings in connection therewith and so that the same should be used for no other purpose''.

7. NINETEENTH CENTURY OCCUPATIONS

During the late 1700s and the first part of the 1800s the industrial revolution transformed England from a mainly agricultural economy to one that was based on new manufacturing processes. This gradual transition included going from hand production methods to machines and the increasing use of steam power. The textile industry was the first to use modern production methods. These changes were reflected in life at Farnley Tyas as manufacturing and trade gradually took over from farming.

The farmers in the village were mainly engaged in dairy farming, therefore grass was the most valuable crop. The farm houses and buildings were in the centre of the village; Hulbert described the village in 1880 'The population is chiefly rural and supplies the town of Huddersfield with milk, butter, meat and other produce of the lovely fields, woods and pastures of this quiet oasis in the realm of manufacturing industry...the population is about 700...''(*p. 266*).

However, when the occupations are analysed in detail it can be seen that involvement in the textile industry, as hand loom weavers and in the early factories, gradually took over from agricultural employment in the nineteenth century. In manufacturing areas such as Farnley Tyas tenter fields were a common sight in large open spaces. Tenters were wooden frames on which cloth was stretched so that it would not shrink or lose its shape while drying after washing. On the 1854 map several tenter fields can be seen and these provide evidence of the scale of textile production at this time.

There is a significant entry in the 1805 Survey (*p.149*) which neatly summarises the balance between the traditional rural landscape and the developing textile industry; steam engines created new industrial conditions: 'Farnley, of which Woodsome forms a part, is however a very compact property and being hilly and interspersed with large woods, the country would be beautiful to the eye if the number of mills and steam engines now about it did not almost continuously contaminate these pleasing features of picturesque beauty, water and air…The old and respectable mansion (Woodsome) thus surrounded by annoyances can no longer be consistent as a fit residence for the owner (Lord Dartmouth) of the property. However, it is these mills and engines combined with the spirit for trade in the inhabitants that stamps an increased value on the estate and therefore it will ill become us to find fault with them".

1821

The 1821 census for Farnley Tyas tells us that out of 157 families, only 36 families were employed in farming whilst many more, 113, worked in trade or manufacturing which would have been mainly domestic hand loom weaving and working in local mills (*Sykes, J. Census and sensibility*). The total population was 900.

1834

Pigot's Trade Directory for 1834 gives the main occupations, other than agriculture, and includes: one blacksmith, one school teacher, two boot and shoe makers, one butcher, two grocers, two manufacturers of fancy goods, three tailors, two tanners, one publican, one wheelwright, one woollen cloth dresser, six woollen cloth manufacturers, one saddler and one carrier. The total population in 1831 was 849.

1841

The 1841 census records the population then was 846. 87 people were engaged in textiles and 65 in agriculture. A brief analysis and outline of some of the occupations reveals:

Farmer 41; Shoe maker 3; Agricultural labourer 24; School master/mistress 3; Fancy weaver 15; Book-keeper 1; Clothier 28; Joiner/carpenter 4; Weaver 19; Drover 1; Cloth manufacturer/dresser 19; Woodcutter/woodman 3; Wool dyer 1; Poor house 3; Wool picker 1; Coal miner/salesman 3; Slubber 2; Publican 1; Factory worker 1; Merchant 3; Lodger 16; Shop man 1; Tanner 2; Apprentice 2; Stone mason 6; Clergyman 1; Tailor 4; Engineer 1; Blacksmith 3; Milliner 1; Butcher 2.

1851

Ten years later the size of the population was much the same: 843. Of these 184 were involved in the textile industry and about 127 were farmers.

Textiles

The variety of textile processes shows the extent of employment in the textile industry.

Hand loom weaver 105; Cloth dresser 3; Power loom weaver 28; Wool carder 2; Slubber 7; Cloth fuller 1; Piecer 5; Bobbin winder 3; Spinner 2; Carter at woollen mill 1; Factory boy 3; Dyer 4; Manufacturer of woollen cloth 8; Woollen labourer/mill operative 2; Burler (removes imperfections from cloth) 5.

Farming

In the agricultural sector people were farm labourers, farmers, farm servants or members of the farmer's family.

There are 53 farms listed in the 1851 census with a total acreage of 920 acres. The average size of a farm was 17 acres; the smallest was three acres and the two largest were Woodsome Hall (50 acres) and the innkeeper, Mr. Kaye had a farm of 45 acres. Many of the farmers who ran smaller sized farms were also hand loom weavers. For example: Joseph Harpin of Hey Fold had a farm of six acres and he was also a hand loom weaver.

Women

Most of the women were described as farmers' wives or daughters. Other than this, 60 women were described as being a house servant or involved in household work, 52 were simply described as 'wife' and nine as 'daughter'.

Children

The village must have been a busy and noisy place; there were 126 scholars in Farnley Tyas in 1851, the youngest was four years old and nearly all were under 13 years old. In addition there were 113 children who were too young to go to school, aged five years and under and babies. Thus children comprised 28 per cent of the population.

The elderly

72 people were over 60 years old in Farnley in 1851: nine per cent of the population. The oldest person was Sarah Harpin who lived on Moor Lane. She was 88-years-old and a former hand loom weaver's wife and she was born in Halifax. Joseph Smith was 80-years-old and a retired butcher. His wife was Susannah Smith aged 70 years. Mark Ibberson farmed 27 acres at Woodsome Lees, employed one farm hand and was a widower aged 80 years.

Occupations other than farming, textiles and housework included:

Coal miner 8; Blacksmith 2; Stone mason 4; Landed proprietor 1; Dressmaker 8; Corn miller/farmer 1; Milliner 5; Brewer 3; Deaf/dumb 1; Shoesmith/blacksmith 1; School master/mistress 3; Butcher/farmer 1; Cord wainer (shoe maker) 3; Clog maker 1; Joiner/carpenter 9; Cattle dealer 1; Wood cutter 4; Highway labourer 1; Pauper 2; Gardener 1; Tailor + tailor's wife 7; Leather dresser 1.

8. THE MILL

Farnley Mill is situated along the Range Dike, in a wooded valley about 500 metres east of Farnley Tyas. It is below the village on the stream between Farnley Tyas and Storthes Hall and now lies in ruins. The 1854 and the 1893 Ordnance Survey maps show the route, Mill Lane, which the villagers would have taken to reach the Mill in the 19th century.

Land Tax returns of 1793 provide the first record of the Mill, when it was leased by William Roberts. It is likely that it was built at about this time according to Alan Brooke. In the 1805 Survey it is described as 'A Fulling and Scribbling mill, built by the Tenants in 1794; under an Agreement for a Lease for 42 Years from May 1794. This Mill is chiefly worked by a Steam Engine as the Water is a very poor Supply from a few small Reservoirs'. A draft lease, recorded in the Agents Letter and Memoranda Book 1804-1810, from the Earl of Dartmouth's agent to Mr Jonathan Senior, the steward on the estate, confirms that the rent was £5 5s. and that the lease was for 30 years from Lammas 1806. Insurance for the mill was to be £1,000 and the tenants were Roberts & Co.

The Mill was one of the first in the Huddersfield area to adopt steam power which supplemented a poor water supply. Dartmouth Estate records make it clear that these

FARNLEY MILL, FARNLEY TYAS, HUDDERSFIELD.

Farnley Mill. A postcard sent to postman John Senior of Far Dean,
Kirkburton in 1907 (Courtesy Farnley Estates)

Copy of a sketch plan of the Mill in 1828,
(Courtesy ArcHeritage Report p.63 fig. 3)

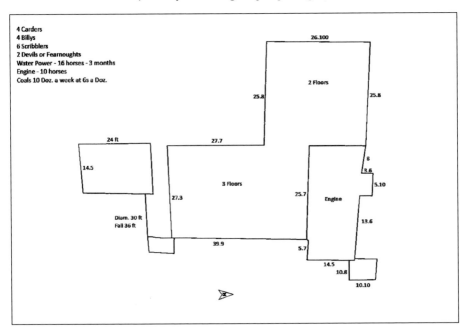

4 Carders
4 Billys
6 Scribblers
2 Devils or Fearnoughts
Water Power - 16 horses - 3 months
Engine - 10 horses
Coals 10 Doz. a week at 6s a Doz.

26.100

2 Floors

25.8   25.8

24 ft   27.7

14.5

3 Floors   8

3.6

5.10

27.3   25.7   Engine

Diam. 30 ft
Fall 36 ft   13.6

39.9

5.7

14.5

10.8

10.10

early steam engines were intended merely to supplement the water power, to prevent stoppage from lack of water during the dry season (*Crump, W. B and Ghorbal, G. 1935 p.76*).

A plan within the 1805 Survey of the Farnley Estate shows the Mill as a single rectangular building with three reservoirs (*ArcHeritage Report 2012 p.3*). The 1828 Survey (*photographs supplied by Alan Brooke*) records the Mill as being on a lease, expiring on the 1st August 1836, and remaining at a rent of £5 5s 0d, to Roberts and Kay. It is described as 'a stone and slate scribbling, carding and slubbing mill consisting of five chambers'. There was an engine house and steam engine of 11 hp and a water wheel of 16 hp. The wheel pit can still be seen (*ArcHeritage Report p. 26 plate 9*).

The machinery inside the mill is listed:

Four carders; Two devils or fearnoughts; Six scribblers; (Steam) Engine-ten horses; Four Billys; Water power-sixteen horses-three months; Coals ten doz. a week at six shillings a doz.

'Water power-sixteen horses-three months' may mean that 16 hp was only available for three months of the year. Low levels of water in the reservoirs in the summer and winter would have resulted in the water power being reduced or only available for short periods of time.

Textile processes

Fulling

The 1805 Survey indicates that fulling was carried out at the Mill. This was a finishing process for woven cloth. The fulling mill's function was to take the clothiers' woven fabric, scour it and wash the cloth in fulling stocks and then to process it to give a dense, felted finish through the action of prolonged pounding in the fulling stocks. The fabric would then be stretched and dried on tentering racks in nearby fields. The mills therefore offered a public service for a fee and were run by a fulling miller who was often a tenant of the local landed gentry family. Lord Dartmouth came to have a major interest in fulling mills during the late eighteenth centuries and early nineteenth centuries.

Though the 1805 Survey states that fulling was carried out at the Mill, all other early nineteenth century reports indicate that it was used for preparatory wool processing activities. The 1828 Survey does not mention fulling and no fulling stocks or drying apparatus were mentioned in the 1850 advertisement for the Mill. Based on the machinery recorded on the plan of the Mill in 1828 we know which textile processes took place there at that time: preparatory wool processing activities.

Scribbling and carding

These were mechanised in the 1770s and were two processes which were usually done in sequence at the preparatory stage of cloth production. The process involved the untangling and opening and straightening of the wool fibres before spinning. This was done by machines with a rotating drum covered in a kind of wire brush (cards); wire teeth were drawn through the fibres to produce slivers. Fearnought machines were cylinders with hooked teeth which thus disentangled the wool fibres. The wool was fed into the machine by the layer-on, or feeder, who was usually a child.

Slubbing

The slubbing billy was used to combine the slivers and produce twist and to wind the product on to bobbins. Slubbing drew out and twisted the textile fibres and joined them end to end on the slubbing billy. The piecer's job was to re-twist by hand any strands of slubbing which broke during the process. Again, children usually did this, often the children of the slubbers. The yarn would then be distributed to clothiers in the near-by village for spinning and weaving (*Giles, C. and Goodall, I.H. 1992*).

Working conditions at the Mill

In the 1830s working conditions in factories were extremely harsh, especially for children. Young children often worked long hours in dangerous and accident-prone jobs. Mill owners and manufacturers considered that reduced working hours would give advantage to foreign competitors by slowing down the running of their factories and making products more expensive. They thought that children aged seven to 14 were more capable of long continued labour than those aged 14 to 21. Joseph Kaye at Farnley stated in 1834: 'Small children are better adapted for piecing than larger ones...the labour is not great but requires them to be in continual motion".

Campaigners for reform, such as Richard Oastler, struggled for factory legislation against the employment of children in factories. The 1833 Factory Act attempted to establish a fairer working day in the textile industry. The passing of the Act did not mean that the mistreatment of children stopped overnight, but there was gradual improvement in working conditions for children. However, the campaign for reform continued and brought about a public enquiry: the 1834 Factory Commission Enquiry. (*Page, C. 2012*).

Joseph Kaye gave the answers to the Factory Commission Enquiry for Farnley Mill (*Factory Commissioners' Report 1834*).The report (*provided by Alan Brooke*) gives a description of life and working conditions at the Mill in that year:

The leaseholders were Roberts, Kay and Dyson. It was a scribbling and slubbing mill for domestic manufacturers, powered by a ten horse power atmospheric engine and a 12hp water wheel on a 'nameless rill'. It was the only mill on the stream. There were 25 employees. These wages would be per person per week.

	Males	Paid	Females	Paid
Under 10 years of age	2	3s. 6d.	1	3s. 6d.
10 to 12 years	3	3s. 6d.	3	3s. 6d.
12 to 14 years	1	3s. 6d.	1	4s. 6d.
14 to 16 years	-	-	3	3s. 6d to 5s. 0d.
16 to 18 years	2	6s. 0d.	-	-
18 to 21 years	1	12s. 0d.		
Over 21 years	8	16s. 6d.		

Four slubbers paid eight piecers; a superintendent or engineer paid four feeders. The piecers and layers-on worked under the supervision of the slubber and scribbling engineer and would often be their children. They were paid from the wages of the adult work people and not directly by the firm. If they were family members they would not be paid at all, as the parent would keep their share for the family expenses and give them spending money if they were lucky.

The working day in the summer began at six o'clock in the morning and ended at eight o'clock at night except on Saturdays, when it ended at five o'clock in the afternoon. In the winter the working day began at seven o'clock and ended at eight o'clock at night except on Saturdays, when it ended at four o'clock. 'Over hours' were not worked: 'parents of children will not allow it'. Regarding punctuality: 'We expect them (workers) at the regular time in the morning and are not very nice (particular) with the children nor are our slubbers...'. Corporal punishments were not sanctioned.

Breaks were allowed during the day: half an hour at breakfast, commencing at eight o'clock in the morning, an hour at dinner, commencing at noon (winter dinner was noon to 12.30 pm), half an hour for afternoon drinking at four o'clock. Machines and the engine stopped at dinner time. During other breaks the machines stopped but the engine was kept running. If a breakdown occurred the workers went home until it was repaired, but they were not paid. Workers enjoyed two days holiday at Christmas, half a day at Shrovetide, one day at Easter, three days at Whitsuntide and half a day at Trinity. Workers were not paid in the holidays, 'the time (was) not made up".

The Mill 'stood still from scarcity of work ...about seven weeks in three years...about a fortnight each year on average...'.

The Factory Commission Enquiry asked for opinions about regulating the hours of factory labour by act of parliament. The enlightened reply of Joseph Kay shows sympathetic attitudes at this mill to the conditions of industrial workers 'In our opinion it will be beneficial not to the children alone but the masters also particularly to those persons who carry on domestic manufacture. Ten and a half and eleven hours of labour appear to be quite enough for adults in a country where more power can be prepared than can ever be required...let the steam engine which cannot feel do the chief part of the labour...and let human beings especially children be spared but not starved in this land of plenty'.

Occupiers of the Mill

In 1836, soon after the Factory Commissioners Report, Baildon, Dyson and Co are recorded as being the overseers (*Halifax Guardian 2nd July, 1836*). The 1838 Farnley Tyas Rate Book lists Fairbourn and Pearson as the occupiers, renting land, the Mill and power from Lord Dartmouth. The extent of the land was 11 acres, three roods and nine perches; the amount to be collected for the Mill and power was £2 1s. 8d. The amount to be collected for the land was nine shillings and nine and a half pence. In an 1842 trade directory Fairbourn and Pearson were listed as scribblers and woollen manufacturers at the mill (*White, W. 1842*).

A comprehensive description of the Mill is given in the *Leeds Mercury* 17th August, 1850 when it was advertised to let.

> To be let a scribbling mill called Farnley Mill situate at Farnley Tyas near Huddersfield together with two cottages and the outbuildings belonging thereto: late in the occupation of John Pearson and Co. There is an excellent steam engine of 14hp with boiler: Stove: five scribblers: four carders: four billys (60 spindles each): Willy: Fearnought and other machinery for carrying on the woollen business to advantage. The Mill is under the Earl of Dartmouth on lease about ten years of which have expired and from its position in the midst of a rapidly increasing manufacturing district is well worth attention. If preferred then the machinery: steam engine etc. will be sold. For rent or price and further particulars apply to Mr. Fairburn, Royd House, Mirfield.

The Mill lease appears to have been purchased by Herman Geissler, a fancy woollen manufacturer, aged 35, who was born in Frankfurt. He was married to Harriet, aged 27, who was born in Kirkburton. They lived at the Dean in Kirkburton and they had one son, aged five years. Harriet was the daughter of William Carter, a fancy woollen manufacturer who also lived at the Dean, Kirkburton (Carter Mill, in Kirkburton, was a small woollen mill dating from the 1840s and various members of the Carter family continued to run the business until the early years of World War I). As well as operating Farnley Mill, Geissler also took over Carter's business after his retirement in the 1860s. Geissler died in 1880 and was succeeded by his son, William Carter Geissler.

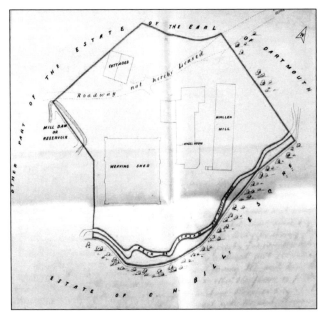

1874 plan of the Mill
(Courtesy ArcHeritage
Report p.65 fig.5a)

1893 Ordnance Survey
map (Courtesy ArcHeritage
Report p.67 fig.6)

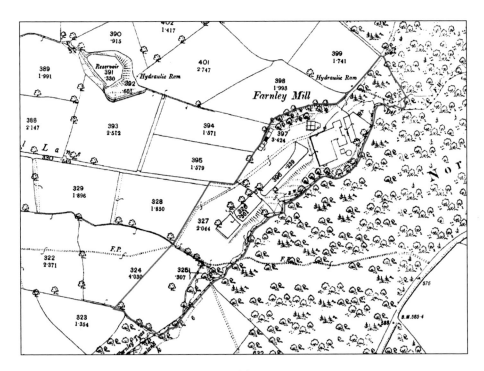

A report in the *Huddersfield Examiner* on 22nd July, 1865, p.7 describes an accident at the Mill.

On Monday afternoon Harriet Horne, aged fourteen years, residing at Birchillbridge, and employed at Farnley Mill, belonging to Mrs. Fairbairn, of Mirfield, met with an accident. She was working at a spinning frame, and had taken an end up at the end of the frame. She was going back again when she touched the box of an upright shaft with her clogs. Immediately she had done so the box fell down, and her dress was caught by the shaft, and she was taken round. She sustained a fracture of one leg, but fortunately escaped any further injury.

The reference to a spinning frame is evidence that the focus of production appears to have changed after Geissler took over, with spinning and weaving being introduced for the manufacture of fancy woollens (*ArcHeritage Report p.5*). Mechanised spinning and weaving were introduced to the woollen industry in the 1820s and 1830s, though take-up was relatively slow until the 1850s, and handlooms continued to be used widely in the manufacture of fancy woollens. It is unclear whether Geissler's company continued to provide processed yarn to domestic weavers, or concentrated on production of their own goods (*ArcHeritage Report p.5*).

An indenture (contract) of 1874 between William Walter, Earl of Dartmouth, and Herman Geissler related to a lease of the Mill, waterwheel, cottages and outbuildings, for a term of 33 years from May 1874 (*Leeds Archives*).

There is a reference to 'the old shaft and two drums which pass through the old mill'. The indenture states that Geissler 'would in the first year...expend in building improvements and in constructing a new reservoir'. The plan depicts the woollen mill, the weaving shed and the location of the wheel house. A report in the Huddersfield Examiner on January 1st 1876 states that 'the trade of the district has been flat so far as the manufacturing interest is concerned, but the building trade and those branches connected have been very brisk, extensive additions having been made to ... Farnley Mill..."(in 1875). It seems that Geissler did invest in building improvements and the 1893 Ordnance Survey map does show a much larger building. In 1854 there were four small reservoirs to the west of the Mill and in1893 only three were depicted. This may indicate that water power was decreasing as steam power, which required less water, took over. The new reservoir, mentioned in the 1874 lease, may be the one shown in the 1893 map north of Mill Lane. Water from this reservoir may have been taken into the east end of the mill to increase the poor water supply. The steam engine would also require water from the reservoirs (*ArcHeritage Report p. 5*).

Herman Geissler was listed as 'Woollen manufacturer' at Farnley Mill in the 1879 Huddersfield and District Directory and 'Hermann Geissler and Son, Woollen Manufactures' appeared in *Kelly's Huddersfield Directory* of 1881. Herman Geissler died the following year and his son, William Carter Geissler, was assigned the Mill for 10s.0d. In 1886 it was conveyed to William Henry Armitage, accountant of Huddersfield, 'upon certain trust for the creditors of William Carter Geissler'. This suggests that Geissler was facing bankruptcy at the time (*ArcHeritage Report p. 6*). On 13th February, 1886 the machinery from the Mill was advertised for sale in the *Huddersfield Examiner,* 'Woollen machinery, material and yarns etc.'. The machinery included condensers, scribblers, carders, hand spinning mules, twisting and winding frames, 36 power looms, tentering machine, four fulling stocks, two washing machines and a great deal more. The stock of material, woollen and worsted yarns etc. was also advertised for sale. A separate sale on 10th April advertised a steam engine, steam boiler, shafting, gearing, steam, water and

Sunken base of gas holder
(Courtesy ArcHeritage Report p.44 plate 28).

gas piping and gas works, also a 'nearly new' condensing engine of '35 horse power'. The sale of the machinery suggests that no other tenant was being sought; its remote location and its small size made the mill uncompetitive with larger mills in nearby towns and villages (*ArcHeritage Report p. 6*). There are no clear records that Farnley Mill was occupied after the sale of the machinery in 1886, though the 1893 Ordnance Survey map does not show it as disused. It is shown as disused on the 1906 map and also on the 1916 map.

The photograph of the Mill on a postcard mailed in 1907 shows a two storey, square, flat roofed building of stone construction with a large chimney on the north side (*ArcHeritage Report p.21 Plate 1*). The 1923 *Farnley Tyas Rate Book* records 'Here are derelict buildings and disused reservoirs'. Demolition took place gradually; maps from 1932, 1948 and 1964 show steadily decreasing levels of building; by 1964 very few structures were shown and after this time the area is shown on maps as woodland. It is likely that stone from the Mill was removed for other building works.

Gas plant

A gas company was founded in Farnley Tyas in 1861 in which 'Lord Dartmouth, F. Thynne esq., and the Rev. C. Wardroper were shareholders, together with the leading gentlemen of the place…the village dwellings are nearly all lighted with gas, the good dames finding it 'cheaper nor candles'…' (*Huddersfield Chronicle 20th June, 1863*). The church and the school were also lit by gas. A half-yearly meeting of the gas company, held in the school room, was reported in the *Huddersfield Chronicle* on 13th February, 1864 which again mentions the reservations held by the women of the village 'The introduction of gas into this village has completely overcome the prejudice which the old farm-dames had against it and in favour of candles…the works are at Farnley Mills, from whence the gas has to ascend all the way to the village, which makes it perhaps the purest and brightest gas in the district…'.

A 'dastardly and malicious' act was reported in the *Huddersfield Chronicle* on 14th May, 1870. 'An evil disposed person caused the loss of a large quantity of gas from the gasometer at Farnley Mill, occupied by Mr. Geissler…a plug was taken out…a large quantity of gas escaped. A reward of £5 0s. was offered for the discovery of the 'miscreants'.

The gas works at Farnley Mill are shown on the 1893 map as a circular structure which could be the base of a gas holder. This is still visible on the site.

On the 1893 map there is a small square building which was probably the retort house where the gas was produced. Before this time lighting at the Mill would have been from candles or oil lamps. The gas works were included in the sale of 1886 (*Huddersfield Examiner 10th April, 1886*). The Kirkburton Gas Light Company took over the supply of gas to Farnley Tyas from the mill gas works in 1884. After this time the gas plant would have been used only to supply the Mill, or perhaps it was redundant (*ArcHeritage p.8*). The gas supply contract for Woodsome Hall is dated 1869.

The Mill cottages

It is likely that the two cottages next to the Mill were built at the same time as the original Mill. The 1828 Survey describes 'Cottage of 3 rooms rented by John Pearson' and 'Cottage of 3 rooms (rented by) John Milner'. A 'stable and cowhouse' are also mentioned, as well as five closes of land: 'Rushy Close, Wheat Close, Mellar Close, Little Ox Pasture and Car Clough Ing…'. The closes consisted of 11 acres, three roods and 19 perches. This land and the cottages were jointly leased for £15 4s. per year. The 1838 Rate Book records two houses at Farnley Mill, one leased by Henry and John Pearson and the other by John Pearson.

From 1841 there is census information about the occupants of the cottages which makes it possible for us to imagine, to some extent, the lives of those who lived so near to the Mill. It is likely that the overseer, or manager, of the Mill lived in one cottage and that a worker lived in the other. In 1841 John Pearson, an engineer aged 45, lived in one cottage and Henry Pearson, a slubber aged 25 lived in the other. John Pearson's wife was called Martha, aged 45. Benjamin Pearson, aged 20 also lived in the house. Martha Carter, aged 15 and Joseph Dodson aged 13 also lived there and were listed as scholars. In the second cottage, as well as Henry Pearson the slubber, there lived Sarah Pearson, aged 20 who we may deduce was his wife and Ann Pearson aged one who we can deduce was his daughter. Employment details are given for the head of the households but not for family members.

In the 1851 census more interesting details are given regarding relationships within the family and employment. In 1851 the 'Ingeoneer' is 40 year old George Dyson who was unmarried and born at Lepton. In the other cottage lived Jonathan Marsh, carder, aged 41, born in Wooldale and married. Hannah Marsh was his wife, aged 37, born in Wooldale and her occupation was 'Household work'. They had a large family with four sons, John aged 15 who was a carder, Alfred aged 11 who was a scholar, Jim aged two, born in Sandal and Dan aged eight months, born in Cumberworth. There were three daughters: Lydia, aged 13 who was a piecer, Ann, aged nine and Mary, aged six who were scholars. Other than those mentioned, all the family was born in Wooldale.

Roberts & Kay   —   Farnley Mill —

Bushy Close	2.2.14	M. Cottage of 3 Rooms rented
Wheat Close	1.1.31	A. by John Pearson - Cottage
Off Mellar Close	2..20	P. of 3 Rooms John Milnes -
Little Ox Pasture	2.3.19	P. Stable & Cowhouse
Car clough Ing	2.3.15	M.

11.3.19

£15.4.5 .

Also a Stone & Slate Scribbling Carding & Slubbing Mill consisting of 5 Chambers. Engine house & Steam Engine of 11 horse Power - & Water of 16 Horse Power on Lease expiring 1 Aug 1836 at the Yearly Rent of —   £5.5.0

1828 lease (photograph supplied by Alan Brooke).
View into the cellar of the western cottage
(Courtesy ArcHeritage Report p.37 plate 25).

In 1861 the Mill manager was Joseph Wood living in one of the cottages. He was aged 50, born in Lepton and married to Elizabeth, aged 53, born in Hoyland and described as Mill manager's wife. In the other cottage lived a woollen carder, aged 34 and born in Marsden. His name is unclear. He had a wife, aged 30 who was born in Saddleworth and is listed as a woollen carder's wife. They had a son and a daughter, aged three and one. The eldest was born in Saddleworth and the youngest at Farnley Tyas.

In 1871, three households are listed. In one cottage lived Henry Woodcock, described as 'overlooker at woollen mill'. He was married, aged 31 and born in Austonley. His wife was Ann Woodcock, aged 24. Her occupation is given as a warper and she was born in Kirkburton. They had a daughter, Emily, who was two months old and born in Kirkburton. In another cottage lived Benjamin Carter who was an engine tenter in a woollen factory. He was aged 53 and born in Kirkburton. His wife was Mary C. Carter, aged 50, born in Kirkburton and listed as an engine tenter's wife. They had one child, Wright, who was a scholar aged six and born in Kirkburton. Another household consisted of William Thorpe, scribbling engineer, aged 39, born in Lockwood. Hannah was his wife, aged 40, with no given occupation and listed as having been born in Huddersfield. They had three sons and one daughter. The eldest daughter was Ann E, aged 12 and born in Kirkheaton. She was a scholar and a half- time factory hand as was their ten year old son, Alfred. John, aged six, was a scholar and Michael was three years old. Michael, John and Alfred were all born in Lepton.

There must have been a number of cottages on the site at this time; (*ArcHeritage Report p. 65 & 66 Fig 5a and 5b*) 'all those several cottages…situate near the mill…now or late in the tenure or occupation of John Fairburn's representatives".

In the 1891 census the number of rooms in a house is given so we know that one of the cottages had three rooms. In it lived Herbert and Sarah Carter, aged 30 and 27 respectively. They had one child, Annie, who was one year old. All were born in Kirkburton. The other cottage was unoccupied. This date is after Farnley Mill went out of use in 1886. The 1911 census records Isaac Eyre, aged 79 and a retired farmer, living at Farnley Mill along with his wife Annie, aged 54. She worked 'at home'. Their dwelling house consisted of five rooms. Their son, Charles, a mechanic, and their daughter Blanch, a tailoress, lived with them. The cottages were occupied for some time after the Mill went out of use.

The 1907 post card shows what appears to be a vegetable garden to the west of the Mill, between the reservoir and the footpath and the 1923 Rate Book records 'House and garden' at Farnley Mill and 'Land, extent 3r 11p' at Farnley Mill, both leased by Albert Roberts.

Anecdotal evidence suggests that the cottages were occupied until soon after World War II. But they gradually disappeared. There must have been some remains visible in 1961 as the Ordnance Survey map for that year depicted their outline. They do not appear on the 1964 map. Now only the cellar is still visible.

The history of the cottages gives us a glance at the lives and occupations of those who lived there. They all worked in the woollen mill at varying functions of the textile processes. They came from a wide area in the region to work at the mill, once an active and thriving community, though now abandoned and deserted.

The Wesleyan Chapel

9. CHURCHES

The Wesleyan Chapel

Hulbert in his *Supplementary Annals of the Church and Parish of Almondbury* (1885) stated that for over 100 years meetings of the Wesleyan Methodists had been held in the houses of the inhabitants because there was no chapel in the village; they were frequently held at the house of Mr. William Johnson Shaw who was a stalwart of the Nonconformist cause. The Wesleyans held a bazaar to raise money for a chapel and this, together with subscriptions, raised £300. It was then felt that the building of the chapel could begin. The expected cost was £500 and a long lease of 999 years was obtained from the Earl of Dartmouth. The first sod was cut on 30th May, 1884 by Mrs. Deborah Shaw, 'in the presence of the few who were friendly to Methodism' and the new building was officially opened in April 1885. The chapel was built on Woodsome Road at the entrance to the village from the east with seating for 116 people. At that time Woodsome Road was a relatively new road, made by the Earl of Dartmouth, from Woodsome and the Kirkburton road. The chapel was one of the later buildings of the Methodist movement; the Holmfirth Methodist Circuit celebrated its centenary in 1910 when the Farnley chapel was only 26 years old. At that time it had 18 actual members, although more would have attended and there were 50 Sunday school scholars.

Mr Frederick Green was the chapel superintendent for more than 50 years. When he died in June 1969, aged 85, his son John took over. He was not only superintendent, but also organist, Trust secretary and Sunday school teacher. When he died all hope for maintaining worship at the chapel seemed to die with him as there were now only three members. One of the last remaining members was Mrs. Hannah Green who, in 1970, remembered chapel life in its hey-day 'We used to have the chapel right full...ladies came in their Victorian dress...there were hansom cabs and trains going from station to station...I remember the laying of the foundation stone...it's a very sound building...we used to have to carry water from the village pump every time we had a tea party...'.

In 1970 the Circuit Superintendent, the Rev. W. F. Burton said that the chapel was no longer required 'It was beyond the means of the remaining members to maintain' (*Huddersfield Daily Examiner 15th May, 1970*). It was auctioned in May of that year when the ground rent was £1 15s. a year. Outline planning permission had been granted for the erection of one dwelling on the site which had an area of about 411 sq. yds. The chapel included a vestry and a cellar. At the auction, bidding started at £500; only three people made bids and the church was sold for £1,100. Prospective buyers had been warned that 'The building shall not be used for the manufacture, distribution, sale or supply of intoxicating liquors, nor for any purpose in connection with gambling...nor as a public dance hall'. The principles of Methodism were maintained. Thus the life of the 85 year old church came to an end. The buyer pulled down the church and built a house (*Huddersfield Daily Examiner 20th May, 1970*).

St. Lucius' Church

St. Lucius' church was built in 1840 and before that time the people of Farnley Tyas walked to the Parish Church of Almondbury. We can read in Hulbert's *Annals of the Church and Parish of Almondbury* (1880) p.70 a reference to the middle of the sixteenth century when alterations were made to the church in Almondbury so that all parishioners could be accommodated. The church was divided into quarters 'then lots were cast, where every quarter of the Parish should sit when they came to church, to avoid contention... Honley, Farnley and Meltham quarter in the North side...'.

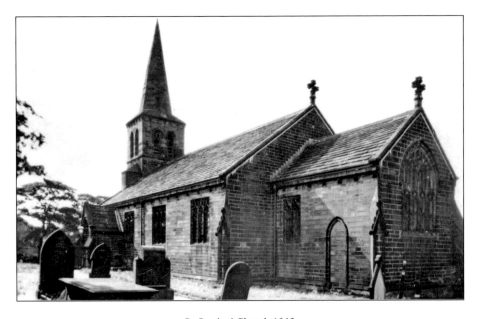

St. Lucius' Church 1913
(Courtesy Farnley Estates)
St. Lucius's Church 2015

However, Farnley people found that Almondbury was too far to travel to church, especially in the winter months. An early mention of this difficulty can be seen in the 1805 Survey (*Dartmouth Estate1805 p.150*). It was important to build a church in Farnley Tyas as,

> The inhabitants of Farnley are now...numerous and as their place of worship (Almondbury Church) lies at a distance and is, in the winter months, much neglected. It was thought proper by us to suggest to the principal inhabitants that we had every reason to think his lordship would encourage any plan they might propose that had for its object the building and endowing of a small chapel for the use of Farnley,Thurstonland and Brockholes.

The growing population in the nineteenth century, due to the increasing use of power-driven machinery and high employment in the textile industry, meant that more churches would be needed. In the Dartmouth Estate records various letters can be read which relate to the early plans for the church.

There was support from the inhabitants for a church to be built in the village: a letter dated September 1833 shows the Earl of Dartmouth acknowledging receipt of a letter from Jonathan Senior, his steward, petitioning for a church in Farnley Tyas. It was signed by the churchwarden, overseer, constable and many of the tenantry. The proposed church was supposed to be at least two miles from the nearest churches/chapels. A letter from the Bishop of Ripon, dated March 1837, to the Earl of Dartmouth sanctioned the Earl's intention of erecting a small church in the township of Farnley. In 1834 there had been revised plans for the church: it was to be lengthened and a gallery for 42 children was to be added.

Lord Dartmouth was applauded for his intention of building a church: a letter from W. Pearce (who was in his Lordship's service) dated September 1834 gives insight into relations between the Lord and his tenants. 'The noble and benevolent intention of... giving your Farnley tenantry the great convenience of having a church in their village is greatly to be praised and they will all I trust duly appreciate it! Such solicitude is too seldom entertained by noble landlords towards their dependants!...I shall rejoice to use the sacred structure raised, in a place, where thirty years ago, the inhabitants might be considered semi-barbarians!'. However, before the church was built there is a record that services were being held in the village. There is an inscription in the 1835 Book of Common Prayer, held at St. Lucius' church, which reads 'Elizabeth Leigh, Royd House 1840. This prayer book was purchased by I. L. for the use of the Clergyman when Divine Service was first commenced at Farnley Tyas in the Schoolroom A. D. 1837' (*Lawson, J. and B. in Mallinson, C. H. and Warwick, G. M. eds.1990*).

Although the fourth Earl of Dartmouth was the founder and builder of the church it is likely that the original idea and planning came from the Reverend Lewis Jones, Vicar of Almondbury, who set up 18 churches and their parishes from the ancient parish of Almondbury. A form of enquiry into the building of additional churches in populous parishes elicits the following information: the population of Farnley Tyas in 1837 was 849. The estimated cost of the building was £1,350 with spire, it was to be endowed with £1,000 and it aimed to accommodate 500 in pews and free sittings. At least one third of the church was to be free sitting for the poor. Pews rents from the remaining were to go to the repair fund which was already established at £67 10s. It was proposed to let the sittings at a rate of 3s. 0d. to 5s. 0d..

The church was dedicated to St Lucius, the first Christian king of Britain. It was erected at the expense of William, fourth Earl of Dartmouth. A directory of 1838 records 'A handsome church is now building here, in the Gothic style, at the cost of two thousand pounds by the Earl of Dartmouth, who intends to endow it with a yearly income for the incumbent. It will have upwards of 500 sittings, and a spire of 80 feet'. (*White, W. 1838*). It was the first of the churches in the Parish of Almondbury to be erected in modern times by private benevolence. The Earl was patron of the church and a very generous supporter. The architect was Robert Dennis Chantrell, who was also resonsible for St Mary's Honley, St Paul's Armitage Bridge and Leeds Parish church. The foundation stone was laid on 17th May, 1838. A letter dated 1840 from the Earl of Dartmouth's agent, informed the Earl that the church was almost complete, except for the internal painting.

A vicarage was not built at that time and part of Woodsome Hall was set aside for the use of the incumbent. The vicarage was built in the village, half-way down Manor Road, between 1861 and 1871. It appears in the 1923 Rate Book as being owned by the Earl of Dartmouth and occupied by the Reverend John Archibald Ashley whom local people still remember. The rent was £39. According to anecdotal evidence the vicarage was a lively place during his incumbency as he had three teenage daughters and he was a man of ability and enthusiasms, which included Esperanto. The Reverend Charles Oswell, who was Chaplain at Storthes Hall, was the last vicar to live at the vicarage. He retired in 1977 and the vicarage was sold and three houses were built in the garden.

There is uncertainty as to how much the Dartmouth family used the church. Some records state that the church was built for the tenants; the Earl and his family still drove across to Almondbury church on Sundays. On the other hand, villagers recall that the Dartmouths used the church when they were living at the Hall and that there is an old stone path leading from the Hall, past Keeper's Cottage, up Field Lane and to the church.

The Reverend Thomas Minster was the first incumbent, assisted by a curate, the Reverend H. F. Beckett. Thomas Minster was a strong supporter of the Oxford Movement which was founded in 1833. It was a movement of high church Anglicans who wanted to reinstate lost church traditions of faith (*Mallinson, C.H. and Warwick, G.M. eds. 1990*)).

The church has some interesting features. The window in the centre of the east wall of the chancel (the area around the altar) was installed in 1856 by the second Vicar of Farnley, the Reverend Cutfield Wardroper. He lived at Woodsome Hall; the path from the Hall, across the park and through part of Carr Wood to the bottom of Field Lane has been known over the years as Wardroper's Way. The window in the church was dedicated to the memory of William, the fourth Earl of Dartmouth. Matthew, Mark, Luke and John are depicted in bright colours. The west window in the tower vestry shows Christ as a shepherd and was erected by the tenants of the Earl of Dartmouth in 1864 to the memory of Frederick Thynne who was agent for the Dartmouth estate for 36 years. The south window in the chancel has the sad inscription 'Erected by four orphan children to the memory of their parents, 1862'. (*Mallinson, C. H. and Warwick, G. M. eds. 1990*)

Hulbert described the church in 1880 'The church contains two aisles, with seats 70 in number, accommodating about 400 persons. There is a neat small organ and a stone font. The pulpit is at the south side and the desk for reading the lessons close by the organ on the north. In the tower, which is surmounted by a plain spire, is a clock, facing towards the west, towards the village...there is no other place of worship in the village...the tower serves as a vestry and has one bell...'. Hulbert describes the spire as 'a beautiful object rising at the western end...' (*p.265*).

In 1899 the church terrier recorded few possessions: a silver chalice (a standing cup used to hold holy wine during Holy Communion), a paten (a small plate of silver or gold used to hold the bread for Holy Communion), a flagon (a pitcher used to hold the wine during Holy Communion) and an alms basin (a plate on which the offering received at a church service is presented at the altar).

Over the years several restoration works took place. Hulbert states (*p.263*) that 'the inhabitants had formerly a gallery in the Parish Church...'. He describes the 'taking away of the Galleries' in 1872 and 'making the whole nave free...for ever'. Some restoration was undertaken in 1880 and the church was reopened in December of that year. The expense was met by a sale of work, opened by Mr. Willaim Leigh of Royd House. The church was refurbished in 1904 when new stalls, pews and screen in limed oak were installed. Also in 1904, three aisles were created instead of the original, single, central aisle. In 1951 the roof, gutters and spouts were restored. Internally, the pavings in the centre aisle were renewed, the woodwork stripped, limed and waxed and the organ overhauled. The pulpit was moved back from the chancel opening and the plaster in the chancel was removed, revealing attractive stone walls. In February 1951, the Bishop of Wakefield preached at a service of thanksgiving. In 1972, the roof on the south side of the nave was completely renovated; the roof on the north side of the nave was renovated in 2007. Pews at the rear of the church were removed in 2010 to create a community space. On the south wall a new inner door was built in 1995; it was dedicated to the memory of John Sykes of Slaithwaite who purchased the Farnley Estate from Lord Dartmouth in 1968. The churchyard surrounds the church and extends to 4,200 yards. It is especially beautiful in the spring when it is carpeted with snowdrops and, later on, daffodils and bluebells. The first burial took place on 3rd January, 1841, for a seven month old child.

The single bell which Hulbert referred to in 1880 was superseded, in 1956, by a loudspeaker system which broadcast a peal of bells. In 1973 this was replaced by three new bells and these completed the chime of four. A fifth bell was added in 1975 (*Lawson, J. and B. in Mallinson, C. H. and Warwick, C. H. eds. 1990*). The first organ in the church was lent by William, Earl of Dartmouth at Easter 1851. The present organ is of two manuals (keyboards) and was built by Peter Conacher of Huddersfield. A strong musical tradition was upheld for many years: the accounts for 1928 show an expenditure of £34 0s. for the choir and music, when the total remaining expenditure for the whole church was £39. There was a choir, consisting of 12 members, until the 1950s.

Church bazaars were, as ever, popular. In 1901 a two-day bazaar was held in the schoolroom. The sewing class, the junior sewing class, the Vicarage, the men, all had stalls and there were many more. There was, naturally, a bran tub! The refreshment stall and the tea room were 'under the effective management' of 21 people.

The church records that in 1917, 32 men from the parish were fighting in the Great War and three others had been killed. In August 2014 a memorial to the men of the village who died in World War I was erected next to the Golden Cock. Ultimately five men died and their names are inscribed on the memorial, W. Johnsey, W. Lodge, E. Price, A. W. Rothery and G. E. Shaw.

Due to the declining population in the village it became clear in the late 1970s that no full-time Vicar would be appointed and it was agreed that union (or reunion) with Almondbury would be acceptable. In 1982 the united Parish of Almondbury-with-Farnley came into being; the Vicar of Almondbury became the incumbent of the whole Parish, including Almondbury, Farnley Tyas and Thurstonland. This was superceded in 1987 by the Team Parish of Almondbury-with-Farnley Tyas. (*Mallinson, C.H. and Warwick, G.M. eds.1990*). The church is now in the Diocese of West Yorkshire and the Dales.

World War I memorial next to the Golden Cock

Village school showing the master's cottage.

10. EDUCATION and the SCHOOL

Background

Before the nineteenth century there were very few schools in England. Most of those that existed were run by the church, for the church, and stressed religious education. Very few children in Farnley Tyas would have attended a school at this time. However, during the latter part of the nineteenth century and early twentieth century several Acts of Parliament were passed which eventually established compulsory education and raised the minimum leaving age to 14 years.

In 1870 the Forster Elementary Education Act was passed by Parliament. The Act meant that attendance at school was compulsory, in theory, for children between the ages of five and ten years. But there were exceptions such as illness, if children worked, or lived too far from school. Children aged between ten years and 13 years who were employed had to have a certificate to show that they had reached a required educational standard.

In 1880 the Elementary Education Act introduced compulsory attendance at school for all children aged from five to ten years. Attendance officers visited the homes of children who failed to go to school. In 1893 the minimum leaving age was raised to 11 years under the Elementary Education (School Attendance) Act. In 1899 the Act was amended to raise the school leaving age to 12 years of age. The Education Act of 1918 raised the school leaving age to 14 years (*http://www.educationengland.org.uk*).To summarise: the minimum leaving age was raised successively to 11, 12 and then 14 years by Acts in 1893, 1899 and 1918, respectively.

During the nineteenth century these developments and improvements in the state provision of education must have had a great effect on the school at Farnley Tyas. From the late nineteenth century increasing numbers of children would have been attending school in the village and fewer would have been working in the fields and in the textile industry.

The first schools in Farnley

As early as May 1806 a school was first proposed for Farnley Tyas 'a day school for fifteen poor children and a Sunday school for children that work...' (*Agents Letter Book 1804-1810*). In May 1807 it was reported by Mr. Pearce, Lord Dartmouth's agent, that the Lord would pay £15 a year towards a school for teaching children to read. The children had to go to church at Almondbury with the master on Sundays. The parishioners would provide money for the expense of the Sunday school and the parish would also build a school room and find a house for the master if Lord Dartmouth would contribute a little wood for heating the school room to which Mr. Pearce did not agree '(giving) £15.0.0.in May will be quite liberal enough without giving bearing timber which would be £40 or £50 more...'. In May 1809 it was reported that 'some of the subscribers are shuffling in their payments...' which had to be enforced.

In 1818 The Report of the Select Committee on Education of the Poor stated 'At Farnley Tyas a Sunday School contains 80 children; and a day school in which 70 attend' (*www. connectedhistories.org*).

We can read about an early National School in Farnley 'before the erection of the church, in 1840, in Farnley Tyas the village had a National schoolmaster in holy orders whose name was the Reverend Sam John Hillyerd' (*Hulbert, C.A. 1885 p.16*). He was at Farnley between 1821 and 1823. Thus, well before the passing of the Forster Education Act in 1870 there was church provision for schooling in the village. Mr. Hillyerd was a minister in the Church of England and he was 'a brilliant preacher'. We know that there was a Free

Children at the turn of the century. With teachers, probably Edwin Sutcliffe and Miss Clara Cotton.

Edwin Sutcliffe's gravestone in
St. Lucius's churchyard

School in the village in 1834 as it is listed in Pigot's Directory of that year. John Hewson was the master. Another early mention of the school is found in a Directory of 1838 'The Earl allows £30 a year to the school master for the education of 30 poor children' (*White, W. 1838*).

However, everything did not always run smoothly at the national school. In a letter to Lord Dartmouth, dated December 1845, his agent wrote 'I regret to hear that Calvert, the schoolmaster at Farnley, is going to leave....it arises from pecuniary embarrassment...'. It seems that Lord Dartmouth had lent the schoolmaster £50 to pay off his debts but this money was 'lost'. The agent wrote to the Vicar, the Reverend H. P. Beckett, in January 1846, expressing his regret over the matter 'I regret to hear so bad an account of Calvert in pecuniary matters...'.

Later in the century education in Farnley was not confined to the national school or to the free school. There is a note, written about 1866, stating 'there is a cottage attached to Bradley's house used as a mechanics evening school conducted by Joe Wood' (*Agents Letter Book 1804-1810*). This is likely to have been the building near the top of Manor Road on the north side, known as 'Suzie's cottage'. Its last occupier was Susannah Bradley who died during the second World War. The cottage now forms part of adjoining cottages (*Beaumont, D. M. 1985 p.38*).

Children and teachers in the village from 1841 to the present.

The 1841 census shows that Farnley had a population of 846, of which 220 were children aged ten years or under. 20-year-old Robert Bransby was the school master who lived in the village. There were two schoolmistresses: Eliza and Hannah Hewson, aged 20 and 45 respectively, who also both lived in the village. A Directory of 1842 (*White, W. 1842*) suggests that there were two 'academies': one run by Robert Bransby and one run by Hannah Hewson.

At the time of the 1851 census Farnley's population was 843 and of these 126 were identified as scholars (15%). The youngest scholar was four years old and the eldest was 16; three scholars were 14 years old. The population included a schoolmistress, Eliza Sugden, who lived at Woodsome Lees and was 40 years old. Her sister, Sophia, aged 32 also lived at Woodsome Lees and was a teacher of music. They were both unmarried and Eliza was the head of the household. Another schoolmistress was Mary Brook, aged 21, who lived in Farnley Tyas. Her husband was William Stansfield Brook who was the schoolmaster in the village. He was 25 years old. They were both born in Leeds.

In 1859, Henry Pilling Battersby was master at Farnley Tyas school. The year of his appointment is not known but an article in the *Huddersfield Chronicle*, 5th February, 1859 recounts an unpleasant incident in which he was involved. A boy aged ten years, George Henry Midgley, had kicked a girl called Emma Garside at Sunday School. This was reported to Mr. Battersby 'who gave the young urchin a sound thrashing with an ash plant...it was found that his legs, back and arms were discoloured by the beating he had received'. Mr Battersby was charged with assaulting the boy. 'The bench remarked that it was unpleasant to have such cases brought before them...the master was quite right in endeavouring to keep the children in order, but in this case he appeared to have used excessive violence'. It was recommended that Mr. Battersby should pay the expenses, which he did.

In 1871, Joseph Scott was the master and Mrs. Ann Scott was the mistress (*Kelly 1881*). In 1879 Joseph Scott was still the school master, Martha Eastwood was the school mistress and Ann Scott was the infants' mistress (*Huddersfield and District Directory 1879*).

In 1897 Edwin Sutcliffe was the master and Miss Clara Cotton was the mistress (*Kelly1897*). Edwin Sutcliffe must have been a busy man because he also ran the Working Men's Club and the Yorkshire Penny Bank on Mondays from seven to eight in the evening. In 1917 he was listed in Kelly's *West Riding of Yorkshire Directory* as an Officer of the village – Clerk and Collector. The 1923 Rate Book records him as living at the school house, which consisted of a house and garden, and was owned by the Earl of Dartmouth. He and his wife, Emmeline, must have had a sad life as they had three sons who all tragically died when young. Humphrey in 1912, Norman in 1914 and Harold in 1916.

Around 1911 Edwin Sutcliffe became ill and vacated the post of school master. Mary A Bramley was head teacher from then until 1927. Subsequently the head teachers were: A. L. Brazier and M. L. Hirst (1927-1929), B. Wainwright (1929), Miss Booth (1932), Freda Farrand (1949-1974), Penny Bradshaw (1974-1991), Anita Hirstle (1991-1998), Alison Hughes (1998-2008), Alison Black/Armitage (2008-2012) and Claire Minogue from 2012 to the present.

The present school

It was not until after the church was being built in 1838 that progress was made in the building of the present school, when the Countess of Dartmouth ordered the building of a school for the village children. Thus the church and the school were built at the expense of the Dartmouth family. The school remained the property of the Dartmouth family, who visited regularly. A schoolhouse was constructed for the master and his family, with adjoining schoolroom to accommodate about 100 children. Separate playgrounds for girls and boys surrounded the schoolroom and at each end of this were the offices. A porch at the front of the school held coats (*Sykes, A. 1970*).

Management

Management of the school was vested in 12 parochial church councillors of the Parish of Farnley Tyas and the church agreed to grant the school £119 per year and to maintain all external repairs both to the school and to the schoolhouse. The agreement was made for 50 years but after only two years the maintenance was found to be too expensive.

In 1904 the school passed into the control of the Education Committee of the West Riding of Yorkshire. The Rate Book for 1923 records that the Earl of Dartmouth owned the land, buildings and school premises and that the occupiers were the managers of Farnley Tyas National School. The rates to be collected were 14s. 0d. and the rent was £3. Under the Education Act of 1944 the school became an aided school which meant that the basic running costs were paid by the local authority. The church paid a contribution (15%) towards the building works. This was revoked in 1957 as the school had become too great a financial burden on the small village community and its church. It then had controlled status; it received no money from the church. This meant that the school was state funded but a foundation or a trust (governors) had formal influence in the running of the school. In 1970 the management was vested in four church councillors, one county councillor and one parish councillor. During the 1970s the vicar would go to the school once a week to talk to the children. In 1974 the school ceased to be part of the West Riding Authority and became part of Kirklees. With this change-over in local government, the school became a first school, known as Farnley Tyas C. of E. (Controlled) First School. The age range then became five to ten years and the school became part of the comprehensive, three tier, Shelley High School pyramid, with all children leaving at ten years for the next stage at Kirkburton Middle School. At the present time (2015) of the total of ten governors, two are representatives from the church, including the vicar, two are staff governors, including the head teacher, two are parent governors, one is from the local authority and the rest are co-opted members.

The building

After 1870, when the Forster Education Act paved the way for compulsory education for five to ten year olds, the school suffered from a serious lack of space due to the increasing numbers of children attending the school. The original school consisted of the main hall and the adjoining junior classroom. Later the infant room was added to accommodate growing numbers.

The school log books give a fascinating and day-by-day account of the activities of the school, the reports of the Inspectors, improvements to the building, curriculum details, attendance, health and progress of the children. The first log book was opened in 1864.

In May 1882, Her Majesty's Inspector (H.M.I.) wrote in his report,

> This school suffers seriously from deficient classroom accommodation; it is one of the few schools in the district where an effort has not been made to secure such accommodation. There is ample room for a classroom in the playground between the infant room and the front.....the urgent need for this room will, I trust, be brought before the promoters of improvements upon the Estate.

In May 1882 the average attendance at the school was 104. Work was started on the expansion and the infants were accommodated in the senior classroom during the disruption. It was not until May 1884 that the improvements were completed and new desks were installed in the new class room.

In February 1883 the steward of the Dartmouth Estate visited the school to consider repairs to the school yard. In July 1883 a report from the H.M.I. claimed that the porches were no longer large enough to act as cloakrooms because the number of children attending had risen considerably. An additional closet was suggested for the girls and more desks for both mixed and infant rooms. In April 1884 work commenced on the porches and during that year improvements were made on desks and heating apparatus.

Four years later, in 1898, another H.M.I report recommended 'improvements of furniture and apparatus…benches and desks should be removed and their places supplied by low dual desks in the classroom for first and second standards and by desks of intermediate height in the main room for the third standard…the latrines and the playground should also be improved…'.

In November 1888 a lamp was placed at the entrance to the girls' playground. Both the girls' and the boys' playground were repaired during the next decade. The heating system was constantly at fault, though a new boiler was installed in 1899. In 1925 Lord Dartmouth's agent, Mr Eagland, examined the heating apparatus and asked the local blacksmith to repair it as the school was too cold in the winter; damp was reported on the walls. In 1908 blinds were added to the infant room as it was too hot in the summer!

In 1921 an average attendance of 80 children was reported and in 1925 this led to further improvements to the building: the gallery in the infant room was removed, a new floor was laid in the large room and several large old desks were sold and replaced by two seaters.

Attendance in 1936 was 63 and they were accommodated in three classes. Each class had a separate room, but the rooms occupied by the first two classes were small and offered only limited facilities for the development of natural activities. During World War II the windows of both the boys' and girls' cloakrooms were sandbagged and the glass covered with cellophane. The cloakrooms were used as air raid shelters. The kitchen window was boarded up and in 1941 all the windows were covered with anti-blast net which provided protection against flying glass. The porches were to be used as air raid shelters. Fortunately Farnley saw little activity during the war so the shelters were not used.

The school buildings were in a poor state in 1953. This was highlighted in critical report by the H. M. I.

> *this small school, with sixty-one pupils, serves the village of Farnley Tyas with its population of three to four hundred inhabitants. It consists of a hall, about six hundred and seventy square feet, and two small classrooms...they join onto the house occupied by the school caretaker. These premises, which are probably one hundred years old or more, are completely out of date, ramshackle and dilapidated...there is a large hole in the middle of the infants' room...this school could be first class if these miserable premises could be replaced by a new building.*

As a result of this report, improvements to the fabric of the school did take place: in 1957 a new boiler was installed and during the late 1950s there were major improvements to the building which included a new kitchen and new toilets being built, though not until 1961 (*Sykes, A.1970*). Up until 1974 there were three class rooms: the main hall, the middle room and the infants' room. Later in the decade this was changed to two class rooms: the main hall and the infant room with three age groups in each class.

The school and school master's house were built at the same time. The house was recorded in the 1923 Rate Book as being owned by the Earl of Dartmouth and occupied by Edwin Sutcliffe. The rental was £12 10s. and the rates were £3 0s., for the school house and garden. In 1991 it was being used as the caretaker's house; it became incorporated into the school and the ground floor became an infant classroom later on in the early 1990s. When the caretaker moved out the teachers took over the garden and made a pond and wild life area for the children.

Health of the children

The log books regularly report on the poor health of the children. In 1864, Henry Pilling Battersby was master at the school and on 7th November he reported that there was 'considerable sickness among young children in the village'. On 13th February, 1865 he wrote 'many children are at home sick'. Twice in September of that year: 'several of the younger children have the hooping cough'. In 1868 Fred Kaye was dangerously ill with scarlet fever, but thankfully, he recovered. Measles was prevalent. On 15th May, 1868 a poignant entry in the log book reads 'James Abbott in the infant school died rather suddenly after a short illness. He was a quiet and good boy...'. On 10th July 1868 'Frances and Jane Wilson were ill at home with the scarlet fever'. In February 1881 'many children were sick... a slight form of the scarlet fever is prevalent and chicken pox'. This continued until March and must have deteriorated as in October 1881 it was reported that 'owing to the outbreak of scarlet fever the school was closed for an indefinite period'. It opened again on 9th January, 1882. In June 1898 there was a whooping cough epidemic; the medical Officer of Health visited the school but did not think it was necessary to close it.

The 1907 Education Act set up school medical services run by local government. It required that each child in the school was to be medically examined on admission and again at 13 years of age. Health was still poor however; in 1914 the school closed from 20th October until 9th November due to a whooping cough epidemic. It is interesting to note that in 1922 the school closed for a fortnight again due to an outbreak of whooping cough and then it was disinfected. During most holiday periods the school was thoroughly cleaned. In the winter months there were many reports of the extremely low temperatures in the classrooms. For example: on 27th January 1925 'the first lesson after play had to be changed for a drill lesson...to keep the children warm...'. It was important to maintain a balance between warmth and fresh air; the importance of ventilation of the schoolrooms was stressed in 1913 'windows are to be opened allowing fresh air without draughts. The thermometer is to be watched and the ventilators are to be always open. In recreation time doors and windows are to remain open and children are appointed to attend to this...' (*Log Book, October 1913*). A healthy lifestyle was promoted when the children were given lessons on health and Health Visitors examined their hands, head and teeth.

In September 1914 Nurse McCracken visited the school and examined all the children. On 16th September, Dr. Towers examined five newly admitted infants and several non-routine cases in the annual Medical Examination. School nurses visited the school on a regular basis throughout the first part of the 1900s. They came twice a month or even weekly to examine and treat the children. Nurses Hartley, Eastwood, Brook, Garside and Haigh were all frequent visitors to the school. Throughout the 1920s and 1930s there were frequent outbreaks of measles, mumps, chicken pox, scarlet fever, whooping cough, jaundice and influenza. The measles epidemic of 1931 closed the school for two weeks and after this the caretaker burned old maps, pictures and worn out books 'so no infection could be carried by them...'.

Nutrition

The doctor was authorised to recommend extra nourishment, and, if necessary, boots. Throughout the 1920s and 1930s extra food was recommended and provided for some children. In 1928 three month's supply of milk was prescribed for four pupils at Farnley and cod liver oil and malt for two pupils. Dried milk and ginger nut biscuits were delivered regularly to the school. In April 1929 'Winnie Speight received maltine and cod liver oil four times...' and later in the year 'seven times". After the annual Medical Inspection in 1931 Dr. Began and Nurse Garside recommended that 'Derek and Gerald Hawley of Hunter's Nab should receive subsidiary nourishment...'. Altogether, in November 1931, five children received subsidiary nourishment; each family had to pay five pence per week. The extra food must have helped the weaker children to survive in those difficult times; 13 pupils at that time attended the Thurstonland dental clinic.

In 1930 a small electric stove and an aluminium kettle were installed for carrying out subsidiary feeding. Dried milk and tins of biscuits were supplied for each child who needed extra nourishment, the charge being one penny a day. Eventually 12 bottles a day of fresh milk were purchased from Mr. Midgeley, a local farmer, and the dried milk was discontinued. The milk was seen as an important source of nourishment; in October 1947 'Dr. Rennie examined the children regarding the supply of liquid milk'. Under the Free Milk Act of 1946 legislation provided free school milk to all British school children. In addition to this, six children under five were given orange juice and cod liver oil. This had been provided by the government in 1944; six bottles of cod liver oil were delivered on 31st January, 1944. Thus milk, and also orange juice, was delivered regularly to the school and in December 1949 2,000 halibut oil capsules were delivered!

Although a school meals system had been introduced in England in 1906, Farnley school did not provide them at that time. The first mention in the log books of this provision was in November 1928 when 'a notice about children staying to dinner and facilities for same...was sent to Divisional Clerk...'. In 1938 Farnley school provided dinners but only for six children. These dinners were free and were cooked on a gas stove. Finally, in 1943, a gas boiler and porcelain sink were installed in the wash kitchen for the preparation of school dinners and a Mrs. Hoyle was employed to cook meals for the whole school. A supply of crockery and cutlery was sent to the school for use in the 'dinner canteen'. It must have been good news for the children on 19th December, 1945 because on that day they had their Christmas dinner; the Vicar and the school managers were present. The cold winters meant that emergency rations were sent in winter in case the roads became impassable.

Frequent and regular reports of visits by the school dentist show improvements to the care of the children's teeth. For example: on 5th May, 1920 a school dentist visited 'and arranged for several children to go to Honley school for treatment'. In 1928, the school dentist 'examined children aged 6-10 years'. On 31st October, 1946 'Mr. Richardson, the school dentist, visited today and gave treatment to children'. In August and September 1948 Miss Rogers was the school dentist who gave 'dental treatment to scholars'. In 1928 care was extended to the children's eyesight; in September three children attended Honley Wesleyan Sunday School for treatment of defective vision and in 1931 four children attended the eye clinic at Meltham. It was not until 1962 that a need for speech therapy was met; a speech therapist visited the school that year.

Finally we read of an annual immunisation programme at Farnley Tyas: in October 1938 15 children were inoculated against diphtheria. The introduction of immunisation against diphtheria on a national scale during the 1940s resulted in a dramatic fall in the number of notified cases and deaths from the disease, though the log books do not record outbreaks of the disease at Farnley Tyas. In November 1946 'Dr. Pickering, Medical Officer of Health, visited school this afternoon and immunised forty-five children against diphtheria'. This programme took place each year at the school until it became standard practice in the National Health Service in 1961. In December 1938 there was a chicken-pox epidemic. Children suffered from further epidemics of tonsillitis, German measles and severe colds in 1948. Vaccinations against poliomyelitis were introduced in 1956; forms were distributed to parents for consent in March. In spite of these improvements to the care of the children's health, outbreaks of measles, German measles, mumps, chicken pox, tonsillitis and colds were prevalent throughout the 1960s.

The Curriculum

As this was a church school attendance at church on Sundays, both in the morning and afternoon, was compulsory. The schoolmaster punished any child who misbehaved during the service or who played truant.

Strong emphasis was put on religious knowledge at the school and annual examinations were held by the Diocesan Inspector. Throughout its history all the Vicars at St. Lucius' church regularly visited the school and were on the management board. During the early history of the school they taught Scripture. The school log books provide much evidence of this: from 1865 the Vicar, the Reverend Cutfield Wardroper, frequently visited the school. On 28th June, 1865 it was reported that Mr. and Mrs. Wardroper had visited and again on 19th July. In June there was a meeting of the Bible Society in the schoolroom and 'all the children were present.' On 1st November 'Mrs. Wardroper came with Missionary Work'. Religious knowledge was a major part of the curriculum; on 19th January 'the first class wrote on the theme of the giant Goliath'. On 6th July 'the first class to write about the Flood'. The children were regularly taught and examined in the Scriptures. The Inspector's report of 1864 reads 'the state of religious knowledge is not satisfactory, being too mechanical...'. In the next record of 1866, the Report of the Inspectors stated 'the

Scripture knowledge of the children is decidedly better than it was last year'. However, achievement in religious knowledge decreased gradually during the decade and poor attainment in other subjects resulted in a condemnatory report in the school log book of 1872,

> this country school is in an unsatisfactory state...the reading is monotonous where it is not a failure. Writing in the upper standards is poor, in the lower, fair. Arithmetic is weak throughout the school. The general intelligence of the scholars appears not to be cultivated in anyway... not a child in the first class could point out England in the map of Europe...reading and needlework are poor.

It is interesting to observe that at this time, in the 1860s, senior children wrote on slates and the infants made letters in sand. There is a note in the log book for January 11th 1866 the children 'didn't take slates home owing to the wet weather...' Again in 1866: 'Fred Turner (went) back for his slate but did not return...'. The slates often became broken and were replaced in the late 1860s by paper, pen and ink. On 14th January, 1867 'The day was so intensely cold that the ink was frozen in the pens so that they could not write...'. On 17th January 'The cold was so severe that the writing could not be done neatly...'. Lead ink wells were inserted into the desks but proved to be dirty and were later replaced by pot ones.

In the middle of the 1860s the narrow curriculum, which was based on religious instruction, reading, writing, grammar and arithmetic, is reflected clearly in the school log books: 18th July, 1865: 'commenced grammar in the first class...'. On 26th July 'taught some boys in the first class compound multiplication...'.

Welcome excursions to the surrounding country during the next few years must have given the children and the master much pleasure: 'took the scholars to Castle Hill in the afternoon...nearly seventy were present. I had coffee on the hill'. The next year, in 1866, the master took 104 children to Castle Hill. He paid for tea for all the scholars 'the day was fine and the children enjoyed themselves...'. There is a fascinating entry in the log book for 13th April, 1873 which shows the mode of transport in those days 'took the children to Castle Hill in the afternoon. The infants taken in two carts to the Hill where all had tea...'. The children and the master would not have seen Victoria Tower as we see it today; it was built in 1899 to commemorate Queen Victoria's jubilee.

Extra subjects were gradually added to the curriculum from the 1860s. Mr. Henry Pilling Battersby was the schoolmaster in 1882 and he 'taught grammar, poetry and geography as class subjects'. The children must have welcomed frequent singing lessons. 'Mrs. Wardroper visited the school and heard singing lessons...'. On 12th May, 1874 Mr. Henry Pilling Battersby made a choice of 12 songs for the children 'and heard them say through...'. In June he taught them the round 'Sing we together...'. These lessons occur regularly during the 1880s. English literature was on the curriculum: Byron, Goldsmith and Longfellow (*The Village Blacksmith*) were taught in 1882 but religious instruction steadily declined; in 1913 papers were sent to parents at Farnley asking whether they wanted their children to have religious instruction; three children were withdrawn.

The broadening of the curriculum is reported in many entries in the school log books. In 1913 children were noting wind direction and weather conditions. The value of physical exercise for children's development was starting to be appreciated; in 1900 a local farmer lent his field so that the boys could play cricket and in 1928 plans were put forward for the purchase of a playing field in Farnley. Drill is mentioned for the first time in a log book entry dated November 1905. In June 1925 a log book entry records 'Mr. Walsh, the drill instructor, visited school and took all classes out into the yards for physical exercise despite very hot sun…'. A reassuring entry the next day records that physical exercise was cancelled in favour of a nature lesson 'under the shade of the trees' in a local wood. Physical instruction continued to develop during the 1930s: rubber balls, skittles and skipping ropes were delivered to the school in 1933; two years later skittles and wooden hoops arrived. In 1941 swimming lessons for girls began; they went to Kirkburton baths for their first lesson on 15th May; the next day the boys had their first lesson.

The main subjects taught in the 1930s were arithmetic, dictation, composition, English, recitation, history, geography, needlework, games and physical training, singing, drawing and art. The infants studied: Reading and Recitation, Nature Study, Singing and Dramatisation. In 1934 boys in the senior section started to attend woodwork classes at Honley Handicraft Centre.

New curricula often demanded new apparatus: in 1936 a Singer sewing machine arrived at the school and in 1944 a wireless set. There were no facilities for instruction in housecraft so the girls were limited to needlework and raffia work. The boys received instruction in woodwork, bookcraft and weaving. Specialist music entered the curriculum in 1942 when a music inspector visited the school and gave demonstration lessons in singing. Books about music and rhythm were afterwards ordered by the school. A record player arrived at the school in 1960. There seems to have been a high standard of literature teaching, *Pilgrim's Progress, Under the Greenwood Tree* and *Silas Marner* were all being studied in 1943.

The children at Farnley must have been delighted with the opportunities which the village school gave them.

Activities out of school started to take place. In 1921 the children were taken to see a fire engine at work upon a burning stack in the local fields. The vicarage garden must have been a delightful location for a 'Bird and Tree Festival' held there in 1929. The programme included songs, recitations, two plays and country dancing. In the 1920s the children of Farnley school would have been stimulated and excited when they visited Huddersfield Theatre Royal to see performances of *A Midsummer Night's Dream, Julius Caesar, The Merchant of Venice* and *As You Like It* by various Shakespearean companies. Each afternoon of the day following the performance was spent discussing the play. During the following years there were regular visits to the Theatre Royal in Huddersfield to see plays.

Nature walks started to appear in the curriculum; an early one was in September 1942 when Miss Booth took the juniors 'the route was Field Lane to the woods at the end of the lane…to collect and study autumn foliage and fruit…'. Another walk mentioned 'senior scholars were taken for a nature walk this afternoon…the route was Mollicar Woods, returning via Farnley Hey…'. This was in April 1946. Mollicar Woods was a favourite destination for these walks and they are frequently mentioned in the log books. The children 'collected specimens of insects and creatures living in the pond…'. In 1953 they went 'to observe trees in autumn and they collected rose hips…'. In 1951 some older children went to Huddersfield Art Gallery to see an exhibition of original paintings and reproductions and, in 1952, 31 children went on a school excursion to Chester. Whitby was chosen for the excursion in 1954 when 36 children and 21 adults took part. York was another favourite location for school visits. In 1959 the juniors were taken to Ravensknowle museum.

Lessons on 'temperance' started in 1914. A drawing master visited Farnley every three months from 1922 and woodwork classes for 12 of the older boys were offered in 1927

(*Sykes, A. 1970*). During the 1970s three peripatetic music teachers and a specialist singing teacher visited the school. Every child played a musical instrument.

Future lives of the scholars at Farnley Tyas school

There are only a few references in the log books to the occupations of the children when they left school. Their lives after leaving school must often be surmised though most would work on the farms and in the mills. However we do get an occasional glimpse. On 30th June, 1868 'Eliza Moss has left the school to go to the factory…'. In July 1871 Fred Haigh 'left the school to go as a Clerk into the Goods Department at Huddersfield Station…'. In January 1874 'Jane Wilson…left school to go into Service…' and on 27th June, 1881 the headmaster wrote 'several children are gone to the mill…'. This may have been Farnley Mill, situated below the village on the stream between Farnley Tyas and Storthes Hall.

Examinations

The school was reorganised after the Christmas holidays in 1946. From then, Farnley had two classes: infants and juniors. The senior scholars, aged 11 years and upwards, were transferred to Kirkburton Modern School but throughout its history Farnley Tyas school was able to report good results in examinations. The County Minor Scholarship exams were taken by children at 11 years and they determined whether pupils could proceed to local grammar schools or go to secondary modern schools. Each year several children at Farnley passed this exam. In 1931 two children passed to the grammar school, in 1966 and 1967 seven passed the exam. Kirkburton Secondary School was the destination of those who failed and Holme Valley Grammar School or Penistone Grammar School took those who passed.

Another grammar school in the area was Mirfield Grammar School. Some schools, including Farnley Tyas, adopted the 'Thorne scheme' which replaced and took over from the County Minor Scholarship examinations (The Eleven Plus). The teachers were more involved in the selection process; children were not tested in the same ways; they completed more project work and they progressed at their own pace. The age range of the children became five to ten years in 1974 when it became a first school in the comprehensive system.

World War I and World War II

National and international events were reflected in the life of the school and these give us an idea of what it must have been like to have been a pupil or a teacher at the school during the World Wars. There are only occasional references to the war in the log books but they provide us with a new perspective on it. In 1917 the War Bonus for teachers was increased to £10 0s. and an extra day's holiday was given to the children in December in honour of the gallantry and devotion shown by the West Riding Forces at the Front. More holidays came in honour of King George V's visit to Huddersfield on 30th May, 1918. In July 1919 it was announced that schoolchildren would have a Peace holiday, lasting for one week, in September. On 15th November, the day was taken as a holiday to celebrate the signing of the armistice and from this time, on Armistice Day, 11th November, the children would assemble at 10.50am. A short service would be held and the two minute silence observed.

Echoes come down to us also from World War II and these also give us some feeling for the war as it affected a small village school and its children. During the build up to the war and the escalating world situation, in 1932, a message about the Disarmament

59

Conference was read and explained to the children at Farnley. In August 1939 it was reported in the log book 'owing to the seriousness of the European situation Respirator Practice was held today…'. On 1st September school was closed for a week owing to the outbreak of war, also to allow for the reception of evacuees. When it reopened on 7th September Respirator Drill and Evacuation Practice were taken. These must have been frightening experiences for the children. Their lives were disrupted again on 14th May, 1940 when the Government announced that 'owing to the National Emergency… all schools are to reopen this morning instead of Monday next…'. A short service of Thanksgiving and Dedication was held at the school in September 1943 to commemorate the fourth anniversary of the outbreak of the World War. The service was conducted by the Reverend J. Miller. Finally, in May 1945, peace was announced and the children enjoyed more holiday from school 'school closed at 4pm and will remain closed for the next two days – 8th and 9th May in celebration of Britain's victory over Germany (V.E. Day)'. Although Farnley saw little activity during the Wars, the repercussions from the national conflicts were reflected at the school in its day to day activities.

Attendance

Work

In 1863-1864 Henry Pilling Battersby was master at the school and he often had to fetch unwilling pupils to morning lessons. There were 128 children registered at the school but the average attendance was only 42.

A main reason for the low attendance rates was that the children were required to work on the farms and so they missed school to do this. On 4th August, 1864, Henry Pilling Battersby wrote in the school log book 'attendance is falling off in consequence of harvest operations. The children are employed in the fields to make 'bands"…'. On 6th October, he reported 'the harvest is gathered and children have again returned to school…'. On 3rd April, 1865 'several first class boys are absent setting potatoes…'. On 27th June it is reported 'school thin on account of hay harvest…'. On 11th July: 'many of the children are in the turnip fields…'. Later in the year 'seventeen children absent…some assisting in threshing…' In 1867 'the hay harvest interferes with the school very much…'. In November 1868 'many children are gathering potatoes…'.

It was not until the Elementary Education Act of 1880 that it became possible to enforce attendance at school for five to ten year olds, when attendance officers visited the homes of children who did not go to school. The officers were also regular visitors at the school.

In the late nineteenth century it is clear that large numbers of children were attending Farnley Tyas school; a large number was recorded was in the spring of 1881 when numbers of 104 were reported, in February 1891 the average attendance was 101. In 1897, 150 children were registered at the school; the same number was on the roll in 1917, with an average attendance of 93. In September 1898 the average attendance was 82, even though 'the harvest was in full swing'. But in spite of attendance officers visiting the school on a weekly or fortnightly basis, the school was still affected by seasonal work on the farms. In 1914 it was reported in the log books that attendance was poor 'many children being away for holidays or haymaking…'. In March 1916 'eight children were absent during the week gathering potatoes…'. 'Working on the farms' was again the reason given for the absence of three boys in November 1924. The large numbers in the early part of the twentieth century gradually decreased; an average attendance of 72 was recorded in 1912 (*Kelly 1912*) and 80 was recorded in 1921.

Illness

Another major reason for low attendance was illness. Due to the outbreaks of infectious diseases and other ailments there were many instances of low numbers. In November 1866 'many children were absent from sickness'. The whooping cough epidemic of 1898 brought numbers very low and for example: in August 1924 there was a measles epidemic so 'attendance was very bad'. Even in 1946 when the children's health had improved and attendance had been prioritised there were reports of 'low attendance due to sickness'. In the 1950s and 1960s attendance improved and regularly reached 90 per cent.

Weather

Severe weather conditions were experienced on the hills at Farnley Tyas and these are constantly described in the log books. At 246 metres above sea level, adverse weather must have made the journey walking to school over fields and along lanes very difficult for children without, what we would call, adequate waterproof clothing. The first record recounts in January and February 1865 'low numbers due to a heavy fall of snow…' and 'the same severe weather continues to affect attendance…many children at home sick. Others from a distance are prevented from coming in the deep snow…'. In November 1866 'attendance of the children has been very irregular this week owing to Tuesday being very wet…'. Two weeks later 'attendance thin owing to the wet day…'. On 17th January, 1867 'the average attendance was very small owing to the severe weather…many children have come late in the mornings owing to the bad weather…'. On 9th February, 1880 it was 'a very stormy day…many children from a distance were absent…'. 22nd January, 1926 brought a heavy snow fall and a storm so attendance was 'poor…'. A deep fall of snow in March 1928 resulted in 'only 35 children being present in the morning and 46 in the afternoon out of a total of 73…'. During the early part of the 1930s numbers of children at the school dropped to the mid-seventies and in 1936 numbers were at 66. A heavy fall of snow on 20th January reduced the numbers on that day to 37. In February 1940 school was closed for a week due to 'the heavy snow and impassable roads…".and in January 1941 'only 17 children out of 67 were present due to a heavy snow fall…'. By 1947 numbers had dropped to 52. In 1953 there were 61 pupils on the roll; in 1955 this had increased to 70. Numbers continued to fluctuate around this level but in 1975 the school roll had dropped to 56. In the late 1970s it was about 40. At the present time (2015) 47 children are registered at the school, likely to increase to 54.

During the 1950s and 1960s severe weather did not have the same adverse effect on attendance at Farnley school – perhaps because transport had progressed, winter clothing had improved, the roads were better or perhaps the winter weather conditions became less harsh? From the 1970s no problems were reported regarding attendance which was stated as being 'good'. The attendance officer still went to the school regularly and visited the occasional home where there was a problem. On the whole 'No one was a poor attender' (*Penny Lunn in conversation*).

The log books record many other reasons for the scholars at Farnley school to miss lessons. These evoke a strong feeling for life in the nineteenth and twentieth centuries and remind us how much has changed since those days. For example: on 19th December, 1864, Henry Pilling Battersby reported 'Girls are many of them absent this week assisting in cleaning at home for Christmas…'. On 29th April, 1865 he wrote in the log book 'Numbers lower this morning in consequence of the preparations for the approaching feast…' (Whitsuntide). An article in the *Huddersfield Chronicle* for 21st May, 1864 describes one such occasion, at Whitsuntide, which would have required considerable preparation. Scholars, teachers and friends assembled in St. Lucius' church, according to custom. The children then sang their hymns and an appropriate address was delivered to both parents and children by the Rev. C. Wardroper. Then 'children and friends walked in procession through the village, headed by Lady Dartmouth's Brass Band. Returning to the schoolroom, 150 children were regaled with buns and coffee, after which about 200 teachers and friends sat down and enjoyed a plentiful repast. The school-room was tastefully decorated for the occasion. The entertainments of the evening were varied... interspersed with recitations by some of the scholars...'.

School was always closed for one day to celebrate Honley Feast in September. It was also closed for Royal Weddings and General Elections. Another major reason for the school being closed was for Lord Dartmouth's rent audits which took place twice a year, in November and June. These are mentioned frequently in the log books. In 20th June, 1867 the note is 'the rent audit of the Earl of Dartmouth which is held in the schoolroom...'. On 12th June, 1868 there was 'a holiday in the afternoon it being the rent audit of Lord Dartmouth...'. In other years these were held at the Golden Cock Inn. The Woodsome Flower show on 23rd June, 1865 meant that the children were given a holiday in the afternoon.

The school farm

In the rural village of Farnley it is no surprise that children were encouraged to work on the land. In 1851 there was a school farm at Farnley Tyas. A report in the *Huddersfield Chronicle* on 6th December describes how the boys benefitted educationally from working on the land which did not interfere with 'elementary training in school hours'. Mr. Brook, the schoolmaster and superintendent of the farm gave the report for the Central Committee of the Farnley Tyas Industrial farm 'The work having been pointed out by the superintendent, or by a hired labourer, is voluntarily accomplished by the boys in their leisure hours and to many boys, but particularly those who are occasionally and similarly employed at home, this little farm and its routine of work has had the effect of winning their attachment to the school and its duties therewith connected...as a physical employment its tendencies have been to bring the mind to that healthy tone...to render pleasant the process of acquiring book learning...thus rendering agricultural labour an important branch of elementary training in the education of the working man's child...'. School farms 'prepared youth for active labour without diminishing their intellectual studies' and they promoted the Victorian values of religion, morality and temperance. The farm was 'a considerable success' and produced an 'abundant crop'. The main crops were oats, potatoes and turnips. Each boy managed a part of the farm and procured seed and manure for himself. This led to boys expressing an interest in agriculture and the chemical processes connected with it.

11. THE GOLDEN COCK

The Inn stood on a good site for travellers at a crossroads and on a main route to Penistone: along Butts Road, passing across Farnley Moor, at Farnley Moor End meeting with Hall Ing Road and the old guide stoop (*see p.76*), down Brown's Knoll Road, Stocksmoor Road, Cross Lane...and on to the markets at Penistone.

The architecture of the building comprises: coursed facing stones, large quoins (masonry blocks at the corner of a wall), moulded kneelers (large stones at the foot of a gable end of a roof) and windows all suggest that it was built in the mid eighteenth century.

During the nineteenth century the Inn was a social meeting place for the people of the village. There was a tap room with spittoons on a bare stone flagged floor and wooden seats. Women were not allowed in the tap room. There was also a snug and a 'best' room, all connected by bare stone floored passages (*Mallinson, C. H. and Warwick, G. M. eds. 1990*).

The Innkeepers

The Kaye family

In the 1805 Survey we see the first mention of the Kaye family whose lives were, for generations, linked with the history of the Inn. Ann and George Kaye held the tenancy of a 26-acre holding and farmhouse in Farnley Tyas. The holding was still attached to the inn in 1934.

It fell to George and Ann's son, John Kaye, to open the farmhouse as an inn in 1821. Along with other buildings in the village, the Golden Cock, public house, is included in the 1828 Survey (*Beaumont, D.M. 1985 p.28*).

Under 'Taverns and public houses", John Kaye, was, in 1834, listed in Pigot's Directory of that year as the Innkeeper at the Golden Cock, Farnley Tyas. There is plenty of evidence for his position: The Rate Book of 1838 includes John Kaye as Innkeeper and tenant of land and buildings at Farnley. In the 1841 census John Kaye, aged 40 years, is listed as 'Publican' at Farnley Tyas. He is listed in an 1842 trade directory (*White, W. 1842*) as 'Vict. Golden Cock'. Ten years later, in 1851, he appears in the Census as 'Innkeeper/farmer of 45 acres'; a substantial farm. The duties of farmer and innkeeper were combined. He was married to Sarah and they had six sons and four daughters. It is said that the family was very religious as a large number of religious paintings, prints and also the large family bible were found in the attic of the inn (*Huddersfield Examiner 5th March, 1934*). Their eldest son was called George and he was a butcher, the next son was William and he worked on the farm, the next son was David; he was a joiner's apprentice. Edward, John, Joseph and Susannah were all scholars. Martha, Mary Ann and Sarah Ann were all 'farmer's daughters' so would have worked and helped with farm and household duties.

John Kaye's status in the village was high; he became chairman and treasurer of the Farnley Tyas gas company in 1863.

A tragic report in the *Huddersfield Chronicle* 1st July, 1865 tells how John Kaye, aged 66, met with a fatal accident. 'Mr. Kaye, who was a farmer as well as an innkeeper, was…proceeding to his field with a cart load of sheep nets and stakes, accompanied by his servant boy Wigglesworth. Mr. Kaye was sitting on top of the loaded cart and while proceeding down Field Lane, to the field, the horse took fright. Mr. Kaye was thrown backward off the cart and fell onto a heap of small stones. The boy Wigglesworth ran for assistance and the injured man was removed home where Mr. Dyson, surgeon, of Almondbury was promptly in attendance but all efforts were in vain and Mr. Kaye died…'.

This sad story demonstrates that farming was a dangerous occupation in the mid-nineteenth century and that the unexpected behaviour of horses could have tragic consequences. The report goes on to state the great esteem in which the people of Farnley Tyas regarded John Kaye and his family. He was 'highly respected, not only by the villagers but by all who knew him…few have passed through life more respected and esteemed for his sterling qualities as a master, a husband, parent and friend…'. John Kaye, like most of the tenantry

The Golden Cock (Courtesy Kirklees Image Archive)

Gravestone in St. Lucius's churchyard of John Sydney Senior, publican at the Golden Cock.

on the Farnley estate, was descended from an ancient family who, for generations, had lived upon the same farm and borne the same name from Saxon times. He was praised for his unostentatious manners, kind disposition and warm attachment. As a publican he showed remarkable attributes. 'In his house no tippling was ever allowed and if a man was the worse for liquor, no persuasion could induce him to supply more...'. If a man was spending money which ought to be for his family 'one pint, and one only, would he suffer such a one to have in his house...'. The tribute concluded that he was endeared to the whole village and his loss 'will not soon be forgotten'. His gravestone can be seen in the churchyard of St. Lucius' church.

In the 1871 Census, Sarah aged 69, is listed as a widow and the head of the family. Her occupation is 'Farmer and innkeeper'. So she continued to run the inn and the farm. Still living with her was William, aged 43, a farmer's son; David, aged 49 and a joiner and Edward, aged 34 who was a butcher. It seems that William inherited the inn as he appears in an 1879 trade directory (*Huddersfield and District Directory 1879*) as 'William Kaye, Golden Cock'. There is the same entry in *Kelly's Huddersfield Directory* for 1881. A William Kaye is mentioned in *Kelly's Directory of West Yorkshire* for 1897. It is likely that he is the same William who was proprietor of the Golden Cock. William's son, Joseph, took over the tenancy of the Inn after him. In 1880 Hulbert (*p.265*) stated that there was 'only one inn' in the village.

The Senior family

By 1891 there was a new family at the inn; John Sydney Senior aged 35, appears in the 1891 census as 'Licensed Victualler'. William Kaye aged 63, 'retired innkeeper and visitor' was living with him. A large household was living at the inn; in addition to William Kaye there was John Senior's wife Louisa, aged 34 years and they had three children, Willie, Kathleen and Doris. Willie and Kathleen were two years old (possibly twins) and Doris was six months old. Louisa's mother and two sisters lived there also. One sister, Ada aged 32 was a confectioner while the other, Sarah aged 25, was a mother's help. Two servants were part of the household, Harry Brierley aged 21, was a farm servant and Ada Winstanley, aged 17 was a domestic servant.

The story of the family who lived at the inn continues in 1911. In this year John Sydney Senior was 54 years and his wife was 53. Ada was still living with them and she was now a 'Household assistant'. William, aged 22, was now a teacher in Barnsley. Kathleen, aged 22 and Doris, aged 20 were both still living at home. There was a new son, George, aged 15, who was a scholar. Two servants lived in the home: John Babbins, aged 24, and Bertha Cotton, aged 19 who was a 'domestic servant".

The 1923 Rate Book states that Seth Senior and Son, from Highfield Brewery, Shepley, were the owners of a 'fully licensed house and premises...The Golden Cock Inn also owned farm buildings and land at the Golden Cock. Joseph E. Eastwood was the occupier...'

Norman Grey became the landlord, under the brewer, Seth Senior, in 1929 and he left in 1946 to go to Park Farm. William Redfern followed him in 1947 (*Huddersfield Weekly Examiner 24th May 1947*). He was a keen football player. He was the coach as well as a playing member of the village football team which had its headquarters at the inn. The inn was also the meeting place of the Huddersfield Motor Club.

Sale of the Inn

The Dartmouth Estate sold the inn for £5,300 in 1945. It was bought by Bentley and Shaw Ltd. of Lockwood. Extensive alterations then took place; the tap room and the passages were made into a restaurant and part of the living quarters was converted to a kitchen. After this Edwin Fox became the landlord and he was followed by Peter Midwood. Peter took over the licence, made more internal alterations and extended the car park (*Mallinson, C. H. and Warwick, G.M. eds. 1990*). The Kirkup family ran the business for a time. The Golden Cock is now a tied inn, owned by Punch Taverns.

Rent audits and dinners

During the nineteenth century the rent dinners at the Golden Cock Inn were the most important events in the life of the village and were accompanied by great festivities and feasting. The Dartmouths, in addition to the Farnley Tyas estate, had tenants in the Slaithwaite and Morley estates but the tenants from Farnley would go to the Golden Cock Inn to pay their rent. In addition a substantial dinner was provided 'and served up in a manner for which the family of Mr. Kaye has been for some generations esteemed...' (*Huddersfield Chronicle 11th June, 1853*). In the accounts for 1863 there is an entry 'All the tenants at Farnley Tyas were entertained by J Kay at the Golden Cock'. A description of the dinners is given in an article in the *Huddersfield Examiner* 5th March, 1934 'The dinners extended over three days and consisted of one for the smaller tenants and another for the more important farmers. It was customary for the London agent of the Dartmouth estate to preside over the latter dinner....which involved the roasting of the carcases of one or two beasts.' Lord Dartmouth's tenants, on this part of his Yorkshire estates, numbered upwards of 200. 'The farmers mustered in goodly numbers and paid their rents very cheerfully, enjoying themselves afterwards'. Informal entertainment 'was provided by the tenants themselves' after the dinner. In 1875 a new wing, on which stands the Golden Cock weather vane, was added to the original buildings; this provided a large room on the upper floor for the rent audits and dinners.

In 1861, William Walter, fifth Earl, was very popular with his tenants because he paid attention to their welfare. Lord Dartmouth's chief agents visited the Yorkshire estates to hold the rent audits, but rarely came at any other time. If therefore a tenant wished to make a request or a complaint, this had to be done at one of these half yearly visits – when the tenant paid his rent. After each audit a report was made of all the matters raised, requests etc. – called the Audit Memo. This was submitted to Lord Dartmouth for his information and instructions. So, although he was an absentee landlord, he kept in close touch with all matters concerning his estate (*D. M. Beaumont 1985*).

World War I brought an end to the custom of the rent dinners due to catering difficulties. Instead each tenant received 2s. 0d. in lieu, a practice which continued until the introduction of decimal currency in 1971.

Occasionally the rent audit was held in the schoolroom. The *Huddersfield Chronicle* 13th November, 1869 reported that 'The half-yearly rent audit of the tenants of the Earl of Dartmouth, on the Farnley Estate, was held...in the National Schoolroom. After payment of their rent, the tenants were entertained to dinner at the house of Mrs. Kaye, the Golden Cock Inn".

Auctions

These were also held at the inn. The *Huddersfield Chronicle* of 30th January, 1864 printed an announcement of a sale of wood 'To be sold by auction, by Mr. Eddison, at the house of Mr. John Kaye, the Golden Cock Inn...on Monday, the 8th February, 1863, at Two o'clock in the Afternoon...FALLS OF TIMBER TREES, Polar, Bark, Topwood and Underwood, standing and growing in the undermentioned Woods, in Farnley Tyas and Honley...Halley Wood and low side of Birks Wood in Farnley Tyas...and Hagg Wood in

Honley...'. Another sale of wood 'To be sold by auction, by Mr. Eddison, at the house of Mrs. Sarah Kaye, the Golden Cock Inn, Farnley Tyas' was announced in the *Huddersfield Chronicle* 6th February, 1868.

The Village Gathering

This was a delightful annual event which took place at the inn. It is described by the Reverend Cutfield Wardroper in an article in the *Huddersfield Chronicle* 4th January, 1855. 'According to annual custom the good housewives of this village met and took tea together at the Golden Cock Inn, in the afternoon, to take a retrospective view of their conduct towards each other, as neighbours, during the past year'. This admirable assessment of their behaviour towards each other concluded that there had been no actual 'differings' among neighbours. Marital disharmony had occurred however; there had been 'some little unpleasantness' and one or two wives had 'run away', but happily things had been made up and 'the fugitives had returned to their duties...'. There was only one point which needed 'straitening up' and this was to do with the lending and borrowing of yeast. When a housewife had asked another 'Can yo learn me a bit o'yest...? Some old dames had turned a deaf ear, although it was well known they had 'plenty o'yest ith' heease!...'. This was settled amicably and it was agreed that it should not happen in the next year; Mrs. Kaye served tea with 'all its legs on'. The happy occasion can well be imagined. 'After a few of the first cups the countenances of the good dames shone with the tints of the rose and their tongues were loosened...'. After this their 'lords and masters' were admitted and there was 'a merry dance...'. The innocent pleasure experienced at these yearly gatherings would come to an end after a few hours, sometimes when the wives would say 'We mun goa wome, lad, or else th'fire 'll be yaat...'. The good neighbours would separate, wishing each other a 'happy new yer".

George Eastwood and the Harvest Festival

A frequent visitor at the inn was George Eastwood. He was a colourful character and known as 'the old Frenchman'. He came from one of the oldest Farnley Tyas families but lived in Paris for 40 years where he was a professor of languages. He also wrote poetry. In 1896 he held a secular Harvest Festival at the Golden Cock. The reason for this was that the harvest was so bad that year that the crops were left to rot in the fields. The Vicar, the Reverend Cutfield Wardroper, refused to hold a Harvest Festival in church until all the crops were gathered. One morning in November several of the villagers, led by George Eastwood, went to a corn field, collected a number of the rotting sheaves and arranged them into a stook in the bar of the Golden Cock. A burlesque hymn for the 'service' was composed by George Eastwood in which he castigated the villagers ''Tis for our good the saints all say – Because our souls have gone astray...The skies would clear, the sun would shine If all observed the laws divine...'. Mr. Eastwood and Mr. Wardroper were often at variance and apparently sometimes their arguments and discussions at the inn became quite heated *(Huddersfield Daily Examiner 5th March, 1934)*. Apart from the hymn parody George Eastwood wrote other verses about Farnley Tyas 'The Conservative Gathering' at Farnley Tyas, on the 8th February,1871 which was 'To warn all the people, round Farnley Church steeple...'Gainst Gladstone's political cheating...'. Another poem was called 'A lamentation upon Farnley Tyas", written in 1870, it looks back with regret at the idyllic village which was now disappearing.

12. VILLAGE CHARACTERS

Daniel Frederick Edward Sykes was born in Huddersfield in 1856 and lived for a time at Roydhouse, below Farnley Bank, in Farnley Tyas.

He wrote a scholarly account of the history of Huddersfield in *History of Huddersfield and its Vicinity*, published in 1898, and *History of the Colne Valley*, published in 1906. They are some of the earliest books on the history of Huddersfield and have become an invaluable source of information for later writers. He also wrote four novels.

His story is a sad one. After a brilliant start in life there were disappointments which led to his downfall. His hopes were blighted due to his strong commitment to politics (*Pearce, C. Huddersfield Examiner 18th January, 2001*). His father, Edwin, was a solicitor who was born in Linthwaite. Sykes was a brilliant scholar and won medals at Huddersfield College. He was awarded a law degree by London University. In 1877 he joined his father's practice and when his father died Sykes seemed on course for a glittering career.

There were two political issues which started the decline in his fortunes. The first was Irish Home Rule. He was a member of the governing body of the Liberal party in Huddersfield. Sykes supported the radical wing of the party and did not have the support of fellow liberals on the town council. The second issue arose between 1881 and 1883 when he founded and ran a newspaper, *The Northern Pioneer*, in which he invested a considerable amount of money. In 1883 there was a weavers' strike in Huddersfield and the newspaper became deeply involved in the local politics behind it. The newspaper was moderate at first in its views and urged negotiation, but finally came out on the radical side and when the strike collapsed so did the newspaper.

When the newspaper failed Sykes was ruined financially; many of his legal clients had taken offence at his politics and removed their business from his practice. Between 1883 and 1893 he took to heavy drinking, though later he joined the temperance movement. He was the subject of a bankruptcy petition and so could not work as a solicitor. He turned to writing and, working as a school teacher, went to Cornwall, Ireland and Canada. He wandered about the country and suffered terrible hardships. A report in the *Huddersfield Chronicle* 4th November, 1893 shows that he was sentenced to two months imprisonment with hard labour for neglecting his children while he was a master at Gainsborough Grammar School. The National Society for the Prevention of Cruelty to Children brought the case. Sykes's two sons reported that Sykes 'always came home unsteady…and they had no food to eat for three days…'. The Inspector found Sykes in bed 'suffering from the effects of drink…'.

Sykes returned to Huddersfield in 1897 and attempts were made to reclaim him from heavy drinking. He wrote temperance pamphlets and tried to re-establish himself. In 1898 he brought out his *History of Huddersfield*, funded by subscription and dedicated to Thomas Brooke of Armitage Bridge.

Around the turn of the century he wrote four novels: *Ben o'Bills, Dorothy's Choice, Miriam and Sister Gertrude. Ben o'Bills* is considered to be the best; it is a compelling documentary novel based on the actual happenings of the Yorkshire Luddite uprisings of 1811-12.

The 1911 Census records D. F. E. Sykes as living at Royd House, Almondbury, (Farnley Tyas). At this time he was 55 and his wife, Mary Louise, was 52. They had been married for 32 years. Their two sons were not living with them in their eight-roomed house. Sykes wrote that his occupation was author and that he worked on his own account at home.

Sykes died of a heart attack, after a difficult life, at Huddersfield Royal Infirmary on 5th June, 1920. He was 64, living at that time at Ainley House, Marsden and had been in failing health for some time. He lived for a brief time at Royd House and so can be considered one of the village's famous residents.

John Nowell had a much stronger connection to the village. He was born at Farnley Wood, the family home, on 1st March, 1794. He went to King James' Grammar School, Almondbury. He died on 4th March, 1869 and his wife, Lydia, died in 1834 aged 37. They had one child, John Shearran Nowell, B.A., who went to Emmanuel College, Cambridge and died in 1867, aged 36; he was buried at Farnley Tyas. John Shearran Nowell married Frances Morice and they had one child, Charles J. Nowell who was ten months old in 1861. Hulbert (*1880 p.266*) described Farnley Wood as a 'sweet retreat occupied by the widow of his (Nowell's) son; who with his grandson, is active in all good works".

John Nowell was an eminent early scientist, a colour chemist, historian, agriculturalist, naturalist and manufacturer at Birks mill. This mill, built on the Dartmouth Estate in the early 1800s by a company of 20 shareholders, which included John Nowell's father, was situated between Farnley Tyas and Almondbury. John Nowell was one of the most significant inhabitants of Farnley Tyas in the nineteenth century. When he was a young man he wrote scientific papers for the *Gentleman's Magazine*. He was a friend of John Dalton, acquainted with Humphrey Davy and Michael Faraday and visited them at the Royal Institution in London. (*Hulbert, C.A. 1880 p.450*). He travelled to France and also to America where he made connections with manufacturers who were similarly occupied in the fancy trade. In *Pigot's Directory* of 1834 he is listed as a woollen cloth manufacturer specialising in Kerseymere which was a fine woollen cloth with a close nap and a fancy twill weave. Twill was a type of textile weave with a pattern of diagonal parallel ribs. The 1838 Rate Book records him as living at Wood in a house with a garden and a dyehouse.

The young chemist

From boyhood he had a strong interest in science. An amusing anecdote from 1809 recounts his youthful obsession with chemistry and how he introduced chemistry into the neighbourhood of Farnley Tyas (Easther, A. 1883). Nowell himself recounts that he had succeeded in producing oxygen and hydrogen. These were placed in stone bottles and taken to an inn ready to be exhibited to members of the Meltham book club.

> *The house was crowded with anxious people...there was a large table in the middle of the room and the young lecturer, then only a lad of fifteen, was placed upon it...the room was crowded to excess and the windows blocked up. Taking courage, the young experimentalist proceeded with his work; the combustion of the file and large drops of molten iron...created much surprise; then the bubbles of oxygen and hydrogen...rising to the top of the room and there exploding astounded those who had never before experienced such effects. Carbonic and other gases were exhibited and in fact all went off successfully. Two or three days after, Mr. Nowell senior, was informed of the exploits of his son, which were not at all to his mind.*

John Nowell kept scrapbooks which were similar to journals and recorded his exploits, activities and thoughts (*Nowell, J. 1843*). The documents provide fascinating reading and show his early interest in chemistry. 'When about fifteen years of age he had a strong

Roydhouse, the residence of D. F. E. Sykes in 1911.

The Wood, Farnley Tyas, in 1923. The residence and birth place of John Nowell
(Courtesy Kirklees Image Archive)

inclination for the Study of Chemistry, which was, to some extent, attributable (when a little boy) to a workman, David North, selling a Dying pan. All boys are imitators, and he accordingly amused himself for months with selling pans and kindling fires. This was about 1798. The same habit continued and when a little more advanced in years he obtained a volume of the *Encyclop. Perthensis* and by the study of the article 'Chemistry', he was further stimulated in the pursuit. In 1807 he visited Sheffield and there he saw the furnaces. In the latter part of that year he made his first experiments. Parke's *Chemical Catechism* became his guide and with some difficulty he procured a copy, after which his curiosity became greatly excited.

He built a laboratory in the corner of the garden 5 ft by 4½ ft, covered it over with two flat stones, with the aid of a mason. In this small place he had an air furnace, also a blast furnace. A neighbouring engineer furnished him with a pair of home-made bellows. His chimney was ten feet high. He also had a little forge. He could melt six or eight pounds of brass in his crucible and made many experiments in fusion. He ultimately turned to making oxygen, which at that time was seldom seen in Yorkshire. His manganese however was of poor quality, and initially all his attempts at generating oxygen were ineffectual. At last Mr. England, a druggist of Huddersfield, procured him some of good quality. 'His delight was unbounded in being able to fill a 6oz phial with the gas. Having thus become expert in the production of these, many of the neighbouring Gentlm. and others came to his experiments".

A useful improvement in woollen manufacture

John Nowell gives a description in his scrapbooks of how he had visited a friend who lived in the cotton district bordering upon Lancashire and had inspected the machinery used in the spinning of cotton 'with some attention' and

> compared it with the mode of spinning woollen thread on the usual 60-spindled Jenny; and on reflecting upon the differences ...I came to the conclusion that if in the process of spinning wool into threads, it could be untwined again in the thread, when so drawn, the parallelism of the fibre would be improved, and by this means a finer yarn might be produced.

Nowell pondered over the matter for a long time before he hit upon a simple method of accomplishing this purpose.

> It happened upon Standedge as I was walking home – a ray of light came into my mind, suddenly as lightning, the simple problem was solved instanter and I walked the dozen miles home in a state something like extasy, nor did I rest that day until the experiment was made'. Nowell attributed his 'happy thought' to the 'attenuated (thin) air on the mountain top'.

His idea was 'to crop the band which carries the motion from the wheel of the spinning-Jenny to the roller, which carries the motion to the spindles, whereby the motions of these spindles were reversed and made to turn the contrary way. The finished yarn that could be spun by one twining, when untwined, and twined the contrary way could thus treated be spun to near double the length...'. Nowell described how eventually this process was 'introduced in the place of the Hargreaves' Spinning Jenny, a machine turned by hand, while the former is moved by the power of water or steam...'.

Dyeing by steam

In his journals Nowell describes the distrust of science when applied to manufacturing processes. According to Nowell the attitude of the early manufacturers was 'What good will your science do? Let us have a practical man – a man of common sense'. Nowell goes on to say that many excellent inventions originated with working men, from which the masters and public benefitted, but who remembers their names? However, 'Science forced

Reverend Cutfield Wardroper on his white horse. (Courtesy Kirklees Image Archive)

Cutfield Wardroper and his fourth wife, Jane McGough whom he married in 1900.

its way and is now become the hand-maid of manufacture'. He goes on to say that it was a long time before woollen manufacturers could be made to believe that steam was one of the most constant conductors of heat. Finally prejudice was overcome 'and the mills have slowly filled up with steam pipes'. Nowell was the first in the neighbourhood to introduce the heating of water by steam in the dyehouse. He states that this development came late 'to this neighbourhood and throughout this extensive Fancy manufacturing district".

Spade husbandry

John Nowell was a strong supporter of spade husbandry and allotment gardens, giving advice to Lord Dartmouth and to his agent Mr. Thynne. At a time when there was a great depression in trade, working on the land was seen as a resource for unemployed manufacturing labourers (*Hulbert 1880 p. 451*). There are frequent descriptions in the newspapers of the time of John Nowell's direction and supervision of these activities in Farnley Tyas. As reported in the *Huddersfield Chronicle* 4th December, 1852 he read a long and interesting report respecting the industrial farm. On 27th August, 1853 'a very lucid and edifying paper which our valued friend and secretary, Mr. Nowell, has prepared' was referred to at a meeting of the Farnley Tyas Spade Husbandry Association. Nowell visited Belgium to inspect the field allotments there and learned much about the substances in manures which he applied to agricultural techniques in Farnley Tyas.

Education

Hulbert praises the virtues of John Nowell 'He took great interest in public improvement schemes, especially those relating to education' (*Hulbert, C. A. p. 451*). He was involved in the founding of Huddersfield College and was a member of the Council. He gave lectures and exhibitions about science to young people, was a Governor at King James' School and introduced the study of chemistry into the school. He was also a Latin and French scholar.

Transcription of the parish registers

Towards the end of his life he took up antiquarian and genealogical pursuits. He collected a vast amount of material connected with family history and helped many people in Almondbury to discover their family lineage and ancestry. To help with this he made a transcript of hundreds of pages of the earlier registers (1557-1652) of the parish church of Almondbury. Due to age the registers were in a poor condition but John Nowell completed the task of transcription in July 1864 after about one year of dedicated work. The Huddersfield Archaeological Society passed a resolution of thanks to Mr. Nowell in 1865 for 'this eminent public service".

It can be seen that John Nowell was a scientist of more than local fame who contributed to the development of the local textile industry. His enthusiasm and involvement in agricultural progress in the area and his commitment to the advancement of public concerns made him a resident of whom Farnley Tyas villagers could be proud. He was buried in Almondbury church yard. Hulbert gave him a fitting accolade 'Mr. Nowell was a kind friend and fitting companion; his memory was richly stored with recollections of the past and his anecdotes, given in quaint, homely language, are not forgotten' (*p. 452*).

The Reverend Cutfield Wardroper was the second incumbent of Farnley Tyas church and was vicar from 1848 until 1899. He was born in 1814 in Midhurst and died in 1905 in Hunstanton. He was a frequent and regular visitor to the school in Farnley Tyas giving scripture lessons and leading the religious teaching. Reference was frequently made to him in the school log books and he was for many years chairman of the Farnley Tyas Spade Husbandry and Stall Feeding Association. In the *Huddersfield Chronicle* 21st June,

1851 it was reported that at the Spade Husbandry Festival at Woodsome Hall 'After dinner an interesting address was delivered by the Rev. C. Wardroper, incumbent of Farnley Tyas...'. Along with John Nowell, and supported by their 'benevolent landlord' he was enthusiastic in promoting the cause of spade husbandry, the industrial farm and allotments. He seems to have been a larger than life character and almost a legend in his own lifetime. There are anecdotal reports in newspapers about him from people who remember him in their lifetime. He was married four times, the last occasion being in his eighties to a woman half his age. His wives were: Marie Antoinette W. Per (1819-1844) who had a child, Eugene, in 1843; Jane Green (d. 1859), Anna Warmoll Butcher (1810-1895) and Jane McGough who he married in 1900.

He was recorded as living at Woodsome Hall in 1861; part of the Hall was set aside for the use of the vicar. By then he was a widower aged 46. Stories were told of his extravagant living at the Hall and how he kept his own carriage and pair (a four-wheeled passenger carriage pulled by two horses). Living with him there were two nieces, Frances and Diana, and two nephews, Edwin and Alfred. A visitor at the Hall was Anna Warmoll Butcher. She was a governess, 50 years old and was born in Norfolk. Ten years later, in 1871, Cutfield Wardroper was living at the parsonage and married to Anna. A cook, Sarah Hodgkinson and a housemaid, Sarah Johnson, also lived at the parsonage.

He was certainly an eccentric character who preached rousing sermons which prophesied hell-fire against anyone he suspected of having committed a sin. Apparently he would shout from the pulpit and point an accusatory finger at wrong-doers. A parishioner, C.W. Leigh, wrote about him in 1903 and remembered him from 20 years earlier 'He was then a tall straight man with a thick white beard and very white flowing hair...' (*Mallinson, C. H. and Warwick, G. M. eds.1990*). He was over six feet in height and used to ride around the parish, and to church every Sunday, on a white horse.

His eccentricity extended to his plans for his own funeral. He had a wicker coffin made for himself long before he died and he kept it in the parsonage. When parishioners visited the house they sometimes asked to see the coffin and occasionally one was permitted the eerie sensation of lying in it. But Mr. Wardroper was not buried in the first coffin he made for himself. A niece who came to stay with him died at the vicarage so she was buried in her uncle's wicker coffin. Another coffin was made for the Vicar. When he retired, he moved away from the village, to Hunstanton in Norfolk, leaving his coffin behind. However, he wished to be buried in Farnley Tyas.

An article in the *Huddersfield Examiner* 5th November, 1905 described the bringing of his body from Hunstanton to Honley station where it was placed in the coffin which Mr. Wardroper had designed for himself. Then it went by hearse to St. Lucius' Church where the service was attended by many friends and former parishioners (*Mallinson, C.H. and Warwick, G. M. eds.1990*). The name-plate from the coffin is in the chancel of the church; on it is inscribed his name and the dates of his birth and death.

Other Local People

Many Farnley Tyas villagers donated to the Holmfirth flood victims and they were listed in the *Huddersfield Chronicle* 28th February, 1852. This draws our attention to the distinguished residents of that time who have been mentioned in the previous pages. Altogether the donations raised £31 11s.. Those of special interest are:

J. W. Roberts - £5 5s	*Rev. C. Wardroper - £5 0s*
Jonathan Senior - £2 0s	*John Kaye - £1 0s*
Workpeople of Farnley Mill – 15s	*George Eastwood – 10s*
Servants at Woodsome - 6s	*Master Wardroper - 5s*

13. ROADS

Turnpike trusts were bodies set up by individual acts of Parliament. They had powers to collect road tolls for maintaining the principal roads in Britain, especially during the eighteenth and nineteenth centuries. At their peak, in the 1830s, 1,000 trusts administered about 48,000 kilometres of turnpike roads in England and Wales, taking tolls at about 8,000 toll gates (*Wikipedia.org/wiki/Turnpike-trusts*).

Farnley Tyas village is sandwiched between two old turnpike roads: the Penistone turnpike through Fenay Bridge and the Woodhead turnpike through Honley. Lord Dartmouth invested money in both projects. In 1804 Mr. Pearce complained that the interest on the investment in the Penistone turnpike road had not been paid since 1798 (*Beaumont, D.M. 1985 p. 36*). Later, in 1845 Mr. Thynne wrote that the interest due to Lord Dartmouth on the Huddersfield and Woodhead Road was £8 13s.

The old road to Farnley

We can read an early description of the old route from Almondbury to Farnley which was given by map maker Warburton. He followed that road with his surveyor in 1719. The route from Almondbury to Farnley is detailed:

A house on ye Lt. (Bank Foot).....
Ascend Leasurely Rheidus (Royd House) Wood on ye Rt.
Top of ye Hill (Farnley Bank).
Enter Farnley town end.
A house on ye Rt. & Scattering houses on ye Lt. A way on ye Lt. to it.
Leave Farnley. Open Rt.
A Rd. on ye Rt. To Honley (Farnley Lane)....
Enter Farnley Moor....Descend (Farnley Moor End)

From Farnley Tyas, Warburton's description of the route to Penistone proceeds along Farnley Moor Lane to Farnley Moor End, to the old guide stoop, down Brown's Knoll Road, Stocksmoor Road and Cross Lane on to Penistone *(Crump, W. B. 1949 p.131)*. Another route is described:

In the days of the Kayes the ancient road from Huddersfield went up Almondbury Bank, through Almondbury village, down St. Helen's Gate and over the Rushfield Bridge. Here it crossed the stream and up through Birk's Wood, taking a line right....it went past the Hall before descending to Woodsome Mill' (Holroyd, A. 1993 p.53).

The modern route from Almondbury to Farnley Tyas is down Sharp Lane, up Bank Foot and then right, up the Woodsome Road.

Handloom weavers, the Rushfield Bridge and the New Road to Farnley Tyas

National events took place in 1826 which had repercussions in Farnley Tyas. Most of the cottagers in the village at this time were hand loom weavers who experienced a 'golden age' from roughly 1790 to 1812; entire families were involved with the trade. Many men who had once been farmers turned to weaving and prospered. Goods were sent to sell at the Huddersfield Cloth Hall. But a series of inventions followed which at first assisted the weavers, allowing for the production of larger quantities of finished cloth. Ultimately, the innovations lead to the destruction of the weavers' way of life. (*www.lancastercastle. com/the-lancashire-riots*). In Lancashire power loom riots took place in 1826 protesting against the economic hardship suffered by the traditional hand loom weavers; this was caused by the widespread introduction of the more efficient power loom. In the textile towns of the industrial north wages fell sharply as the factory system was developed. In addition, economic depression followed the end of the Napoleonic Wars in 1815; the price of bread, cheese and meat doubled. (*Wikipedia.org/wiki/power-loom-riots*).

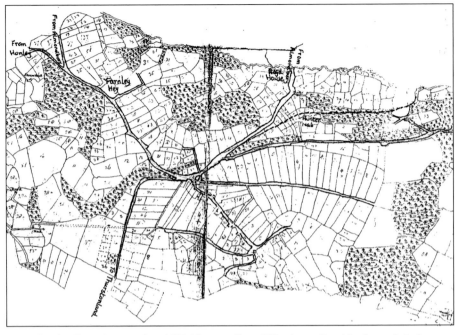

Farnley Tyas. Approx. date 1828. The new line of Woodsome Road is shown dotted.
(Courtesy Kirklees Archives)

Guide stoop at the end of Farnley Moor Lane.

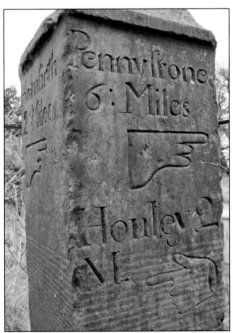

Thus, the hand loom weavers of Farnley Tyas were suffering severe distress. 'When the severe distress of the hand loom weavers came on, in or about 1826, in order to find employment for the operative and manufacturing workmen various improvements were suggested to create employment for the workmen and one of these was the widening of the almost impassable lane leading from Almondbury to Rushfield' *(Easther, A. 1883 p.22).* At a meeting of parishioners to discuss the project a vote was passed to build a new culvert, for £15 at Rushfield Bridge, which at that time 'consisted of little more than a plank'. The Chairman was Mr. E. Roberts and he was entering the unanimous vote on his minute paper when a voice rose from the dense mass of parishioners.

Yo're all a pack o'fooils together; yo care not yah yo rob the public. Fifteen pounds for Rushfield Brigg!! Yo're nowt but a set o'robbers.....Yo're nowt but rogues and thieves. Fifteen pound!! Fifteen shillins sadly too mitch for that; for t'road leads nowwher but to Na-wills' (Nowell's) at t'Wood. Fairnley fooils is bad enough, but Omebury fooils is waar!!

The old man was mistaken as to the advisability of the outlay. The repair of the bridge led to the building of a new road to Farnley which connected the Penistone turnpike road with the village and improved access to the village from Woodsome Hall, all at a cost nearly £4,000. All of this came from a generous gift from William, the fourth Earl of Dartmouth, who provided labour for the famishing poor of the district. This is the road which we still use and call the Woodsome Road.

The actual route of the old road into Farnley is difficult to follow. Crump states that it is likely that as far as Hunter Nab the two roads were in parallel or took the same route. After Hunter Nab it is likely that the old road, which can be seen on the 1805 map and on the 1828 plan, took a route higher up the hillside; the new road was cut lower down the hillside. It is shown, sketched in pencil, on a plan of Farnley Tyas prepared at the same time as the 1828 Terrier, presumably having been sketched on at a later date *(Kirklees Archives).*

The road was referred to as the 'new road' in an article in the *Huddersfield Chronicle* 13th September, 1856 and Hulbert *(p.176)* describes it as 'the new road from Woodsome…to the village of Farnley Tyas…connecting the main road with that village".

An Ancient Mile Stone on Farnley Tyas Moor

At Farnley Moor End a mile stone, or guide stoop, was erected. It states that: Huddersfield is 3 miles; Pennystone is 6 miles; Honley 2 miles; Holmfirth 2 miles. It was erected in 1738 by Jon. Hoyle, Constable and Thos. Bottomley, Surveyor.

We take signs at road junctions for granted but it was not until 1697 that the systematic placing of such signs was put into effect. Why was the stone erected?

Perhaps people had become lost on Farnley Moor. Also, an increase in internal trade and the movement of wool to markets in the seventeenth and eighteenth centuries led to an improvement in road surfaces. These developments made it necessary to mark routes very clearly. Under an Act of 1697 directional posts, or stoops, had to be erected at cross roads to show the mileage to the next market town. It was ordained that 'there be erected or fixed in the most convenient place where such ways joine, a stone or post with an inscription in large letters, containing the name of the next Market Town to which each of the said joining highways lede, upon paine to forfeit by the said Act the summe of ten shillings' *(Huddersfield Examiner 30th September, 1967).* The order was issued by the Clerk of the Peace for the County to Chief Constables who in turn sent it to the Surveyor. On 11th October, 1738, at Sheffield Quarter Sessions, the order contained in the Act was repeated and it was in that year that the milestone was erected. It used to have a sundial on top but that disappeared long ago.

Stone troughs at the bottom of Manor Road. (Courtesy S. Haigh).

Man at Pump. Mr. W. Shaw in May 1947, with the village pump
at Butts Road and Woman at Fountain in 1947.
(Both courtesy Huddersfield Examiner)

14. WATER SUPPLY

The wells

The earliest supply of water to Farnley Tyas came from individual wells, springs and pumps. The Ordnance Survey 1854 map shows a 'trough' to the north of 'water main'. These are likely to be the 'wells public' shown in the extract from an undated map 'Farnley Tyas Water Supply'. (see below)

These troughs, fed by underground springs in the area at the bottom of Manor Road, were the original water supply for the village. They had been buried and were revealed during the demolition of the pump house in 2007 (*Haigh, S. 2007*). Anecdotal evidence suggests that the wells or troughs were used by villagers within living memory.

The reservoir in School Wood and the fountain in the village.

Lord Dartmouth 'caused a great improvement to be made in the village in the matter of a water supply, much to the convenience of the inhabitants…'. This local supply replaced the individual wells, springs and pumps in the second half of the nineteenth century. A report in the *Huddersfield Chronicle* on 23rd November, 1861 provides evidence that the improved water supply was operating by then. It also gives a striking and powerful description of the water source in the centre of the village.

> *A large reservoir has been made on high ground, (in School Wood) from which the water is conveyed to the centre of the village, where it issues from a beautiful fountain and falls into a large trough and cistern, at one end of which cattle can be watered. The area around is walled off, except on one side, and at one corner there is a stately stone-built pillar, from which the water flows copiously (for domestic purposes) through a stag's head, with antlers as large as life. On the top of the pillar is a gas lamp and post which gives light to all around. The lamp is surmounted by a beautiful crown, and the whole is a great ornament to the village.*

But the state of the reservoir and its maintenance were causing concern a few years later, as reported at a Farnley Tyas Local Board meeting. In November 1864 'The attention of the Board was called to the state of the reservoir in the school plantation…'.

The reservoir was surrounded by oak trees and many leaves drifted into the water in the autumn causing the water to have an unpleasant appearance and some people thought the leaves gave it a peculiar taste. Mr. George Shaw expressed the opinion that it was too late to clean the reservoir out as it should have been done earlier in the year when it was empty. He did not think that it mattered if a few oak leaves were deposited in the bottom so long as they did not interfere with the flow of water into the pipes. The chairman, Mr. Gilbert Wilson, expressed the opinion that the Board ought to take possession of the reservoir so that it could be maintained efficiently. Lord Dartmouth had built the reservoir but now the inhabitants should contribute towards keeping it in good working order. The reservoir had not been cleaned out for three years and this at Lord Dartmouth's expense. Gilbert Wilson suggested that the Local Board took on the management; as representatives of the inhabitants, they could, at the right time, pay attention to small defects and keep the reservoir in good order at a small cost (*Huddersfield Chronicle 5th November, 1864*).

In 1880 Hulbert (*p.265*) confirmed 'There has been a plentiful supply of water in public wells, by the paternal care of the noble proprietor".

The Pump House

A key element in this local piped water supply was the pump house. Water was supplied to the reservoir at the top of the village from springs at the bottom of Manor Road. Spring

The reservoir in School Wood
The Pump House. Demolished in 2007. (Courtesy S. Haigh)

water was diverted into a cistern and then pumped through a pipe up to the reservoir at the top of the village in School Wood. From there it was distributed by gravity to the properties in the village in Manor Road. The pump house continued in use until the late twentieth century although it was adapted for a series of different pumps. The water supply system is documented in the nineteenth century plan of the village 'Farnley Tyas Water Supply' showing a line running up Manor Road depicting the pipe to the upper reservoir. The plan depicts the brick 'reserve' or reservoir which was built next to the pump house.

It also documents that the pump house originally had a steam engine. A cast iron boiler would have produced steam for this engine. It is known that this was superseded by a gas engine as a gas pipe was found during demolition. This supplied gas to the engine from a town gas supply in the village. There was conversion to electrical power in the twentieth century, probably around 1945, as shown by the electricity pole at the side of the building. The pumping had to be done on a daily basis and villagers still recall carrying out this work.

Two substantial stone blocks formed the engine beds. When these were removed during demolition a large circular, stone-lined water-filled cistern was discovered underneath the flagstone floor. This cistern, or primitive reservoir, must have been the original supply for the pump, before the building of the nearby brick reservoir between 1850 and 1890, and built in the same period as the pump house itself.

The pump house, built at the end of the nineteenth century, thus provides evidence of a complex and organised system for collecting and distributing water for a whole village. It is significant because it shows the evolution from the relatively primitive stone troughs which were in use in the mid nineteenth century to the electrically pumped, piped supply in use from about 1945. The pump house was built to house a steam engine or pump to supply the village with water via a reservoir and gravity system. Later it was adapted to house a gas engine and an electric pump (*Haigh, S. 2007*).

Local residents report that Manor Road was supplied with water from the pump house. Residents from Church Terrace, Butts Terrace, Dartmouth Terrace, the old chapel and the Golden Cock used a wooden pump outside the Golden Cock until 1939. Later they were supplied by the Corporation. A booster tank was put up on Farnley Moor as the Corporation supply was not adequate.

The reservoir in School Wood supplied water to the village until the early 1990s when Yorkshire Water put a main down Manor Road and made a supply from the reservoir to the village. This water was from a Yorkshire Water supply, not from springs. The reservoir is not in use now as all properties are connected directly to Yorkshire Water mains (*Steven Greaves in conversation*).

Circular cistern beneath demolished pump house (Courtesy S. Haigh)

Farnley Tyas water supply. Extract from undated map in possession of Farnley Estates showing the bottom of Manor Road

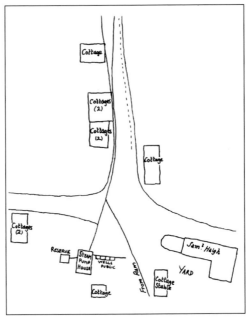

The old brewery on Moor Lane

15. BREWERY

In 1845, John William Roberts, a tanner of Farnley, was planning on giving up his business because he suffered continued ill-health. He passed it on to his son who converted the business to a brewery on Moor Lane. In the 1851 Census Edward Roberts, his son, is listed as the brewer along with his father, John William. An article in the *Huddersfield Chronicle* on 8th October, 1864 shows one of the problems faced by brewers in those times. At a local board meeting it was reported that 'Several complaints were made respecting water being taken from the wells at the bottom of the town, by Mr. J. W. Roberts, common brewer…owing to the general scarcity of water, Mr Roberts cannot obtain a sufficient supply of water from his own reservoirs for his trade purposes'.

It was reported that Mr. Roberts had been fetching water from the public wells in a large barrel during the night and in the daytime. When other people went to the wells in the morning for water for their cattle and other domestic purposes 'they found them empty and were unable to obtain a supply for their most pressing wants'. The Board considered that if Mr. Roberts would restrict his use of the wells to the night and not take any water from the wells after five o'clock in the morning, there would be sufficient during the day for the use of all the villagers. The Chairman of the meeting was Mr. Gilbert Wilson and he agreed to discuss the matter with Mr. Roberts. Hulbert *(p.265)* described the brewery of Messrs. Roberts as 'extensive'; this can be seen on the 1854 map.

In the 1870s Richard Roberts joined Edward Roberts in the partnership and in 1881 two sons of Edward Roberts, John Stocks and James, joined the brewery business. John Stocks Roberts died young in 1897, aged 36, and was buried in St. Lucius' church yard.

The malt kiln, adjoining Moor House, was bought in 1879 and in 1899 Bentley's Yorkshire Brewery bought the business (*Huddersfield Examiner 10th February, 2015*).

In 1902, T. E. Dickinson, mineral water and bottle making manufacturer from Spring Grove took over the business; he bought Moor House and the lands. In the 1923 Rate

Brick reservoir (Courtesy S. Haigh)

Brewery reservoir

Book it is recorded that the Earl of Dartmouth owned the Old Brewery which was occupied by T. E. Dickinson who paid a rental of £8 5s. Dickinson and Son Ltd. were taken over by Duncan Gilmour and Co. Ltd., of Sheffield, brewers. Eventually brewing came to an end later in the 1920s.

The present Roebuck and Holmes building was a mill owned by Harry Haigh who lived at Moor House. The mill produced worsted cloth. It was also used as a commissioning weaving shed; pieces of cloth were sent out to homes for local people to take out the knots (burlers). The mill ceased production in the 1940s. For a time it was a soft drinks factory and then was owned by Farnley Fabrications. In 1993 Roebuck and Holmes bought the building from Farnley Estates and started renovation work in 1994. The firm now manufactures office and shop furniture.

Bottles from Roberts' brewery dating from the late 1800s and also bottles from Dickinson's brewery have been dug up in the vicinity and they show a cockerel image embossed as a trade mark. This symbol presumably shows an association with the Golden Cock in the village.

16. WAR TIME CRASH AT FARNLEY BANK

On the evening of 17th February, 1942 at 10.20 pm. the crew of a Wellington bomber from 460 Squadron of the Royal Air Force was trapped in the blazing and wrecked fuselage of their plane which had crashed on a hillside by Woodsome Road, a few yards from the junction with Bank Foot Road. Sadly, all six airmen on board lost their lives; they must have been killed instantly.

The squadron was undertaking day and night training flights in preparation for bombing raids on Germany and had left its base at Breighton, near Selby, at 7.20pm. The aircraft's defensive machine guns were fully armed. Visibility was poor with a lot of low cloud, but wireless communications had not indicated anything wrong on the flight. The plane was 37 miles west of its intended course when it came down and the pilot may have been flying low to establish his position. It was reported later that there was not thought to have been any mechanical failure; the plane struck a steep hill and burst into flames during a cross country flight at night.

Due to wartime censorship there were no contemporary reports of the incident, but since then several people, who quickly arrived on the scene, or who were affected by the blast, have given descriptions of the accident 'The scene the following morning was witnessed by many Almondbury schoolboys, many of whom later scavenged the area for metal fragment souvenirs' (*Huddersfield Daily Examiner 14th January, 1995 p.11*). Rowland Winn was 16 years old at the time of the disaster and living in a cottage just below where the crash took place "The plane came across the valley and over our house, then we heard a thud…my mother who had gone upstairs to bed, was looking out of the window and said "the woods are on fire".

Two people, Ned Ellis, a tenant farmer who had been out checking on his cattle and Harry Sykes, who was returning home on a path after taking his wife to her work at Storthes Hall Hospital, had narrowly escaped being hit by the falling aircraft. Mr. Sykes was blown over a wall and knocked unconscious by the blast as the plane came down. Two policemen later helped him up from where he was lying in the middle of the road. The doomed bomber first hit a cottage at Farnley Bank, slicing off the roof and demolishing a gable wall. It then crashed sideways into the hillside and burst into flames. The sound of the exploding ammunition from the bomber's machine guns continued well into the next day. Philip Shaw of Butts Way in Farnley Tyas recalled that firemen drew water from a hydrant outside his home before going down Woodsome Road to fight the blaze. He said 'The firemen said they had no chance at all to save the crew' (*Huddersfield Daily Examiner 21ˢᵗ January, 1995 p.11*).

The six airmen who tragically lost their lives in February 1942 were:

Pilot – Sgt. James Henry Ware, aged 20, of Sydney, Australia;
Second pilot – Sgt . Robert Tressider, aged 22, of Coogee, Australia;
Observer – Sgt. William Ashplant, age and origin not known;
Wireless operator – Sgt. Cyril Davies, age and origin not known;
Wireless operator/Air gunner – Sgt. Frederick Dutton, aged 20, of Cheshire.
Air gunner – Sgt. Cyril Dickeson, age and origin not known.

It was reported that the crash was the talk of the village at the time. The cottage was rebuilt and is now known as Wellington Cottage (*Huddersfield Examiner 28ᵗʰ April, 2015*).

On 25ᵗʰ April, 2015 a memorial plaque was unveiled on the wall of the cottage where the bomber crashed; former R.A.F. servicemen honoured their colleagues who had been 'training to help (us) in the war'.

Memorial plaque on the wall of the cottage where the Wellington bomber crashed

17. VILLAGERS' MEMORIES and ANECDOTES

Contributed by Eric Briggs, Pat Cartwright, Peggy and Stanley Dodson, Robert Fardell, Jean Hirst, Jean Stavely, Vera Cocking, Charlotte Mallinson.

In 1838, William Dyson owned a grocer's shop at Town End and in 1923 Ben Woodhouse owned a shop, a house and the post office in the village. The shop was at the bend in the road, opposite the Golden Cock and next to Field Lane. Ben came to the village just after World War 1. He sold groceries and also corn for the farmers. Flour in sacks was brought by Sugdens of Brighouse. It came in steam wagons which used to pull up alongside the shop and crane the flour in. The shop closed in the 1960s/1970s.

Ernest France was the postman. He brought the mail by bike from Fenay Bridge, Dogley and up Farnley Line. It was delivered once a day to individual houses.

Mr. Tom Snooks was the policeman. We were terrified of him! Sydney Fardell was a special constable and he tried to help the crew when the Wellington bomber crashed in 1942. Arthur Abby was another special constable; he lived at the Manor House. Mr. and Mrs. Fardell were caretakers at the Wesleyan chapel.

Norman Grey was the publican at the Golden Cock during the 1930s and World War II. He lived at Park Farm down Manor Road.

In 1923 the Armitage family owned buildings for weaving which were occupied by J. Haigh.

There was a wheelwright who worked between Church Terrace and the Golden Cock and a blacksmith came from Honley on Saturdays, every two weeks, to shoe horses. Two blacksmiths came to the village. One had a shop next to the fountain; he came on Tuesdays. The other worked from the Golden Cock farm and he came on Saturdays. My grandfather shooed horses next to the Golden Cock.

The slaughter house was at the top of Manor Road, on the left hand side, coming up, next to the Manor House. Herbert Turner was the butcher; he lived at the farm, Meadow View, which was two hundred yards from the butcher's shop on the other side of Manor Road.

The brewery was down Moor Lane (now a track). It was in ruins when I was a child; we used to play hide and seek in the old building and gather blackberries there.

Moor Lane is known locally as Crab Lane.

Villagers remember the clattering of hooves on the road as cows were herded from the fields at milking time. The cows used to slow the traffic down.

Gerald Dartmouth used to come in May, when the bluebells were in flower, for the Rent Audits. He used to stay with the Agent on Farnley Moor.

There was a communal water pump next to the fountain and people from Coronation Yard used to fetch their water from this as there was no mains water in Coronation Yard.

There were four cottages in Coronation Yard. The cottages backed onto Manor Farm where the Kayes lived. Two of the cottages were converted to a mistal (for milking cows). The stables backed onto where the bus stop is now. Jim Brown had four lads and he used to bring them to the stables to have their hair cut by horse clippers.

Between Manor Farm and the reading room there is a little ginnel which leads to Coronation Yard where there is a very old manor house barn. Manor Farm is now called Yew Tree Farm.

Farnley Tyas village centre in 1951 (Courtesy Huddersfield Examiner)

Tom Snooks, policeman 1927-1946, with his
mother, Louisa, in1954
(Courtesy Huddersfield Examiner)

Hunter's Nab in 1921
(Courtesy Kirklees Image Archive)

Forty years ago (in the 1970s) only ten families owned their own homes; the rest were tenants of the Farnley Estate. Since then a lot of property has been sold off.

When John Patterson became the Dartmouth agent in the late 1950s, the estate started modernising. The cottages had become run down but government grants were obtained to modernise them. The farmers got grants and they expanded their dairy herds to make money. John Patterson was the instigator for all this.

Farm building conversions started in the 1960s – until then everyone was a farmer. Just in the centre of the village there were at least sixteen farms. All the farms were tenanted. There were two farm tenants at Marsh Lane and one at Ing Head, Stocksmoor. Names of some of the farms were: Poplar Farm, Park Farm, Beech Tree, Croft House, Netherton Farm, Manor Farm, Ivy Farm and Meadow View. All the farms, buildings and land, were eventually sold. First those outside the village and then those in the centre. Shaw Head, where the Kaye family lived was sold off.

I remember when the Mill cottages were standing, but no one was living in them and I remember three dams at the Mill. There was a good solid road for horses, leading from Woodsome Lees to the Mill and on to Brockholes. It went from the Mill, behind Jean Hirst's house, to the brewery, up Moor Lane, past Ivy Farm, joined Brockholes Lane, to Brockholes village, up Lancaster Lane and to the Holmfirth Road.

The old route of Moor Lane used to go past the brewery, across the bottom of Manor Road, behind the cottages and down Mill Lane to the mill.

I remember the full-time gamekeeper, Jackson, living at Keeper's Cottage; the shooting parties were very popular in the 1960s. People came from surrounding villages: Reggie Rippon from Honley, Albert Gill from Thurstonland, Stanley Dodson from Farnley and Ben Woodhouse the grocer from Farnley Tyas.

In 1932 there was a well behind our house at the bottom of Manor Road. It was fitted up with a pump and we got water from there. We were connected with mains water in about 1939. Eric Briggs used to put treatment in the tanks at the pump house and pump the water up once every day.

During World War II, a bomb dropped at Castle Hill.

In 1935 there were big celebrations in the village for the Silver Jubilee of King George V and Queen Mary, also for the Queen's coronation in 1952.

The rent audits were big occasions when the agent, Mr. Eagland, used to come over from Slaithwaite.

We lived in the cottage of the farm at Hunter's Nab. It backed onto the hill and we could climb onto the roof and read up there. My sister and I used to help the farmers, George and Wilf Sykes. They used to give us a spoonful of molasses every day and told us it would do us good. We got food from the farm; we ate well and we were not affected by food rationing during the war. We used to walk to school every day up Farnley Line and we took a jacket potato and beans which were cooked on the stove at school. Potatoes to roast, pies and stews to heat on the stove or in the small oven were carried to school by children in the 1930s.

When I was 14, I worked as a mender at Harry Haigh's mill on Moor Lane. My mother had been a weaver there. I worked there until Harry Haigh came out in the middle of the 1940s.

I used to walk to school from the bottom of Manor Road and on Thursday afternoons we used to walk to Honley to do woodwork. It was held at Honley school by the church. It was in a separate room, above cottages, across the road from the school.

In the summer we used to go, from the school, to play in the recreation ground because there was not much space in the school playground. If there was a special celebration we used to dance round the maypole there. The boys used to play football at the far end. The Whitsuntide walk was a big occasion. I remember it in the 1930s. There was always a band. We used to walk round the village from the school and the church with the church choir. We walked, in a procession, with our parents and people from the village down Manor Road, stopping at the Manor House (Abby's) where we used to sing in the garden and were given a drink of lemonade and one penny. Then we went to the Vicarage and sang there. We used to run around under the big tree in the garden and we used to put on school plays on the vicarage lawn and concerts in the schoolroom.

Miss Farrand was the infant teacher at the school, later she became the head mistress. Mrs. Wainwright was the head mistress when I was at the school.

Winters were very severe then (in the 1930s and 1940s). Children had to walk a long way to school in deep snow drifts. We walked on top of the walls to stop sinking in the drifts. 1947 was especially bad. We had to take gas masks to school for air raid practice though there were no actual air raids.

I lived at Wood Farm, below Hunter's Nab. I used to go to school in a horse and cart from Wood Farm. When I was four I got diphtheria. My grandfather, Willy Kaye, lived at Manor Farm opposite the Golden Cock. My other grandfather, Joseph Edgar Eastwood, was the innkeeper at the Golden Cock until 1925 and my mother lived there when she was a girl. She was born at Croft House Farm, down Manor Road and I remember her talking about Cutfield Wardroper.

We used to walk to Holmbridge for dances and we also went to dances at Farnley Bowling Club. The Bowling Club building was a hospital in Longwood during World War 1. It was brought to the village by horse and cart by local farmers around 1920. The bowling green was built on a bed of clinkers taken from old Farnley Mill.

There was an old custom: when a bride and groom were getting married the villagers used to tie the church gates together during the ceremony. The married couple could not get out until the groom had thrown some money onto the road outside the church yard.

We got electricity in 1928. It came from a cable at Dogley. The first buses came in 1924. they had hard wheels. Many of the villagers used to work at Storthes Hall.

SOURCES

ArcHeritage. 2012. Archaeological investigations at Farnley Mill, Farnley Tyas, West Yorkshire, Survey Report Number 2012/9.

Beaumont, D.M. 1985. The Dartmouth Estate and its management.

Census: 1841, 1851, 1871, 1891, 1911.

Crump, W. B. and Ghorbal, G. 1935. History of the Huddersfield woollen industry. Tolson Memorial Museum.

Crump, W. B.1949. Huddersfield highways down the ages. Tolson Memorial Museum.

Dartmouth Estate. Including Farnley Tyas, Honley and Meltham. Agents letter and memoranda book 1804-1810 (Kirklees Archives).

Dartmouth Estate. Farnley Tyas rate books 1838 and 1923 (Kirklees Archives).

Dartmouth Estate. Farnley Tyas minutes of the Local Board and U.D.C. 1878-1925 (Kirklees Archives).

Dartmouth Estate. 1847. Farnley Tyas tithe award and map (Kirklees Archives).

Dartmouth Estate. 1805. Selected extracts and maps from the 1805 Terrier of the Dartmouth Estate, by Kent, Pearce and Kent (Farnley Estates).

Dartmouth Estate. 1828. Terrier of the Dartmouth Estate (photographs provided by Alan Brooke).

Dyson, T. 1951. History of Huddersfield and district, from the earliest times down to 1951. 2nd ed.

Easther, A. 1883. A glossary of the dialect of Almondbury and Huddersfield. Ed. from his manuscripts by Thomas Lees. Published by Forgotten Books 2013.

Ellis, A. 2006. A history of St. Lucius' church, Farnley Tyas.

Factory Commissioners' Report. 1834. Employment of children in factories 1833-1834. British Parliamentary Papers (provided by Alan Brooke).

Farnley Tyas Community Group. 2008. Farnley Tyas community plan.

Farnley Tyas village website: www.farnleytyas.org.

Farnley Tyas and Woodsome manor court rolls, 1381-1684. Trans. by the Misses Freeman from the records of the Kayes of Woodsome and later the Dartmouth Estate (Kirklees Archives).

Giles, C. and Goodall, I.H. 1992. Yorkshire textile mills 1770-1930.

Haigh, S. 2007. Former pump house. Manor Road, Farnley Tyas, West Yorkshire: archaeological building recording.

Holroyd, A. F. 1993. Woodsome. The place and its people.

Hudson, P. 1975. A study of the West Riding wool textile industry 1750-1850.

Hulbert, C. A. 1880. Annals of the church and parish of Almondbury, Yorkshire.

Hulbert, C. A. 1885. Supplementary annals of the church and parish of Almondbury, July, 1882 to June, 1885.

Mallinson, C. H. and Warwick, G. M. eds. 1990. Aspects of Farnley Tyas yesterday and today.

Nowell, J. 1843. Scrapbooks: local history of Almondbury, science, weather, agriculture and allotments 1843-1867 (Kirklees Archives).

Olde English village faire. 1907 . Woodsome (Huddersfield Local Studies Library)

Page, C. 2012. Nineteenth century life at Lord's Mill. (Honley Civic Society).

Sykes, A. 1970. A history of Farnley Tyas church school 1847-1940 (Farnley Estates).

Sykers, D. F.E. 1898. The history of Huddersfield and the valleys of the Colne, the Holme and the Dearne. Toll House Reprints, Facsimile ed. 1986.

Sykes, J. Census and sensibility (from Farnley Estates).
Trade Directories (Huddersfield Local Studies Library)
Huddersfield and District Directory 1879
Kelly's Directory of West Yorkshire 1897
Kelly's Huddersfield Directory 1881
Kelly's Directory of the West Riding 1912
Pigot and Co's National Commercial Directory 1834
White, W. 1838 History, Gazetteer and Directory of the West Riding of Yorkshire. Vol. 2
White, W. 1842 Directory and Topography of the Borough of Leeds and the whole of the Clothing District of the West Riding of Yorkshire

Log Books
Farnley Tyas C. E. (C.) First School (provided by Claire Minogue).

Maps
Supplied by Huddersfield Local Studies Library, Kirklees Council.
Ordnance Survey map 1854. Surveyed 1848-1851. 6ins. to a mile.
Ordnance Survey map 1893. Surveyed 1888. 25ins. to a mile.
Ordnance Survey map 1906. Re-surveyed 1888, revised 1904. 25ins. to a mile.

ACKNOWLEDGEMENTS
John Sykes and Paul Sykes for providing much information and access to the Farnley Estate
Paul Elgar for a tour of the Farnley Estate
Alan Brooke for information on the history of the mill and newspaper articles
Pam Brooke for inspiration
Steven Greaves and Stephen Haigh for information about the water supply
Jean Hirst for information about the tan house and the water supply
Peter Marshall of Honley Civic Society for editing and support
Claire Minogue for access to the school log books
David Pedley for information about the Dartmouth Estate
Jan Thornton for lending documents and giving information
Richard Wood for information about farm building dates